LEARN SOMETHING NEW

PLAY GUITAR

Publications International, Ltd.

CONTENTS

INTRODUCTION

When you pick up the guitar for the first time, it's easy to feel daunted by the unfamiliarity of it all. Getting past the soreness and blisters of a few long practice sessions is hard enough. But then you have to learn how to tune the thing, memorize all those note names, and work hard at finger coordination too. You also have to strum while playing chords—a technique that involves holding down multiple fingers while playing three or even more notes. What's the best way to get a handle on all of this? Which approach is best for you? After all, there are hundreds of methods out there.

It all comes down to practice. Whatever method you choose, you need to spend some time getting to know the fretboard. Practice. Then practice some more. Then repeat. At some point all good guitarists realize that the key to reaching their goals is to keep practicing.

This book will familiarize you with one of the fundamentals of accomplished guitar playing: chords. They're the building blocks of songs and they will help you think in terms of song structure. There are plenty of guitar chords to be learned—thousands, in fact. But you only need to know a handful to be able to play songs. The chords and chord progressions in this book are the ones you need to start with. We'll look mainly at first-position chords (so-called because of their position at the end of the neck, near the headstock), but the end of each chord section includes additional chord voicings so that you can experiment with them as well.

As you learn new chords you'll get to try them out in simple chord progressions. As your chord inventory grows, the progressions will become more songlike. By training your fingers to move from one chord to another in these progressions, you'll develop the skills to accompany other musicians and perform solo before you know it. The biggest key to success—practice regularly!

The instrument you have decided to learn wasn't invented by a single person or culture. It's the product of centuries of experimentation and inspired invention. Archaeologists have found statues and carvings of guitar-like instruments in Susa, an ancient city in what is now Iran, that date back 3,500 to 4,000 years. Modern instruments evolved from earlier ones like these. As the instruments evolved, their features changed. Body shapes have been round, triangular, and square, with some having hollow resonating bodies and others being solid and flat. Typically modern guitars have six strings. Earlier guitars sometimes had more. Predecessors like the Renaissance lute might have had from 15 to 24.

Modern acoustic and electric guitars are part of a family that includes lutes, mandolins, pipas, balalaikas, sitars, charangos, and hundreds more. Their shapes are simply variations on a design that goes back to prehistory.

The twang of the hunting bow may have been the sound that led to the invention of stringed instruments. The single-stringed instrument seen here is a berimbau, a Brazilian instrument that probably originated in Africa. It is hit with a small stick to produce a buzzing sound. The gourd attached to the bottom amplifies the sound. Its similarity to a hunting bow is unmistakable.

CLASSICAL GUITAR

Modern guitars developed from a classical guitar template. The classical guitar grew from a group of earlier instruments, including the lute, baroque guitar, and vihuela (a Spanish guitar of the fifteenth and sixteenth centuries). In the nineteenth century, a Spanish guitar maker named Antonio Torres Jurado helped give the guitar its modern form. Because of his influence, the instrument is sometimes known as the Spanish guitar. The guitar's strings are tuned E-A-D-G-B-E.

The classical guitar has six strings and a hollow body. It gets its sound from the player plucking the strings with both fingernails and fingertips. Once these strings were made from animal guts, but in modern guitars the strings are made of synthetic material.

The acoustic guitar is a portable instrument that you can play anywhere without worrying about amplifiers or microphones. But while it may have started out as an instrument common to intimate settings like coffeehouses and campfires, the acoustic guitar has benefited from contemporary pick-up technology. From the garage to the arena, the acoustic can go anywhere the electric goes.

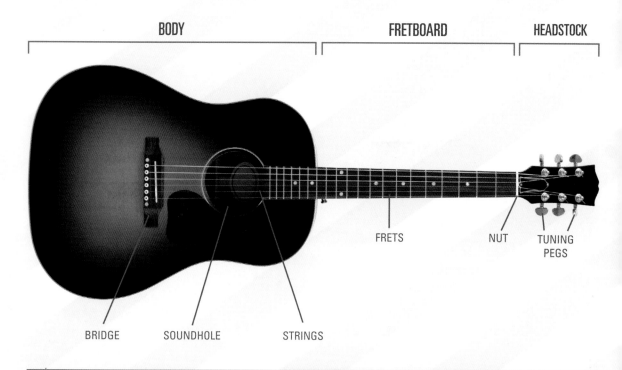

BODY   FRETBOARD   HEADSTOCK

FRETS   NUT   TUNING PEGS

BRIDGE   SOUNDHOLE   STRINGS

TUNING PEGS & NUT

A guitar has six *tuning pegs* that may be positioned on one side of the headstock or three to a side.

The strings are laid over small grooves on the *nut*. This holds them in place.

THE BRIDGE

The strings travel down the neck and go over the *bridge*. On most acoustic guitars the strings are anchored through the bridge with bridge pins. On electric guitars, strings may be fastened to the bridge, the tailpiece, or be run through the body of the guitar itself.

In the 1920s jazz musicians amplified their archtop acoustic guitars with microphone-type pick-ups. These guitars were forerunners to the modern solid body electric guitar we know today. In the 1940s a musician named Les Paul developed the solid body guitar by using a solid piece of wood for the body of the guitar. This gave the guitar more sustain and less feedback when played at higher volumes.

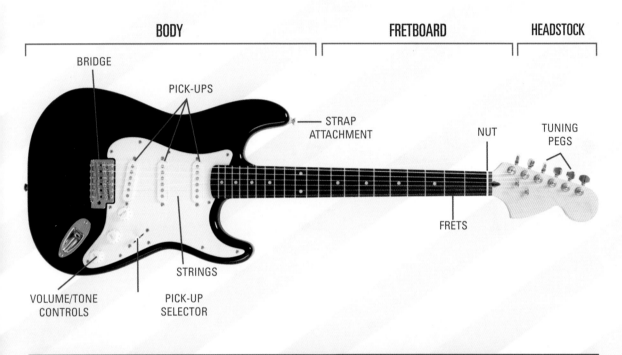

FRET MARKERS

On the side of the guitar neck are tiny dots called *fret markers*. Often there will be two dots on the twelfth fret.

VOLUME/TONE CONTROLS & PICK-UP SELECTOR

Electric guitars and some acoustic guitars are equipped with *volume* and *tone controls*.

On the electric guitars that have more than one pick-up there is a *pick-up selector*. On a Les Paul-type guitar it is located on the upper left side of the body. On a Fender-type guitar it is located near the volume/tone controls.

STRINGS

The diameter of a string—its gauge—is measured in centimeters: the lower numbers designate the thinner strings. Electric guitar players prefer light gauge strings (0.09–0.42) because they are easier to bend. Acoustic strings are heavier. They range from 0.10–0.47 (light) to 0.13–0.57 (heavy). The style of playing often determines the string size the player uses. For example, a finger-style player might use a lighter gauge string while a blues or slide player would prefer a heavy string.

Once you have played guitar for a while you may want to experiment with different strings. Once you settle on a style of playing you usually settle on a particular type of string.

Strings have changed over the years. Manufacturers still try different alloys or types of windings. A recent addition is the coated string—this string has a thin layer of plastic that keeps it free from oil and dirt, and gives the player a better-sounding, longer-lasting string.

Classical guitar players use a different type of string. Their instruments can't support a high amount of tension on the neck, so they use a special nylon string that doesn't require the tight winding of a steel string.

E string ——

A string ——

D string ——

G string ——

B string ——

E string ——

Typically entry-level guitars require strings with ball-ends. These are barrel-shaped beads that fix the strings in the bridge.

PLAY FROM THE GUT?

Steel guitar strings are a relatively new invention. So before steel, nylon, and other synthetic materials, what did musicians use to string their guitars? Three common materials were hair, animal gut (yes, intestines from animals like sheep and cows), and silk.

WINDINGS

As you get to know your guitar, do take the time to investigate string varieties. String type is where your tone starts, and it's not just the gauge that determines that tone. The string construction method, or *winding*, will also have an impact. There are three main windings to consider.

Flatwound This string's winding wire has a rounded square cross-section. Thanks to its smooth surface, these are the least squeaky strings you can buy. Flatwound strings are favored by many jazz, soul, and R&B musicians and any guitarist looking for a warm, mellow sound with lots of tonal range.

Roundwound This string's winding wire is circular. This leaves an uneven playing surface. This bumpiness results in more finger friction and more squeaky, scratchy noise. However, these strings do have a bright, aggressive sound, and are cheap and easy to find.

Ground roundwound (halfwound) These strings also use a circular winding wire. But the winding has been polished down until the surface is nearly flat. They are quieter than roundwounds but not quite as mellow as flatwounds.

STRING MATERIAL

The materials your guitar strings are made from also shape your tone. The way they do this is complicated—every good guitarist has an opinion on how materials shape tone. For now, just be aware that different alloys accentuate different tones.

Three common choices for electric guitar are:

Nickel Vintage older tone. Consistency of tone over the lifetime of the string.
Nickel-plated steel Balanced tone. Bright and articulate attack.
Stainless steel Balanced tone. Less squeaky. Resists corrosion and lasts a long time.

Common choices for acoustic guitar include:

Bronze Clear, ringing tone. Age quickly due to bronze's tendency to oxidize.
Phosphor bronze Warmer and darker than bronze. Last longer due to the phosphor alloy.
Silk and steel Steel core with wraps made of silk, nylon, or copper. Soft and delicate tone. Easy to play.

THE GUITAR PICK

There are many ways to play the guitar. In this book you will be learning to strum chords and chord progressions. Picks are usually used to strum chords, so you should select one that you're comfortable with first.

Hold the pick firmly in its larger section. Be sure the pick is at a ninety-degree angle to the guitar and strum from the top string to the bottom string. Your wrist should be loose enough to strum up and down on all the strings.

USING YOUR LEFT HAND

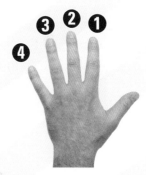

Your left hand holds the notes down. The most important part of guitar playing involves the left hand.

Let's start with numbering the left hand. When you are trying new chords, there are times that your fingers don't actually move to the right position. Try using your other hand to push the finger that doesn't quite fit into position.

When you wrap your left-hand fingers around the fretboard, make sure that you arch your hand so that your thumb is perpendicular and directly behind the neck.

SOUTHPAW BLUES

The instructions and images in this book reference right-handed playing techniques and positions. If you are playing a left-handed guitar, hand and finger positions will appear reversed.

There is a simple logic to the arrangement of notes on the fretboard. Let's look at each string to see how the fretboard works, starting from the lowest note—the open E on the top E string.

Beginning with open E, play the first six notes. They are E, F, F♯/G♭, G, G♯/A♭, and A. Now play the open A on the next string. If you have tuned your guitar correctly, the A on the E string and the open A should sound the same. This is the beginning of a pattern on the fretboard.

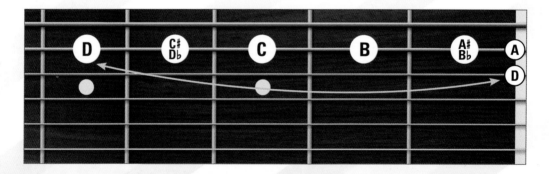

Beginning with open A, play the first six notes. Then play the open D on the next string. As with the two A notes, the two D notes should sound the same.

On the E, A, D, and B strings, the fifth fretted note is the same as the open note on the next string. On the G string, you only go up four frets.

BEYOND THE FIFTH FRET

The notes on each guitar string are arranged like those on a piano keyboard: as you move from neck to headstock, each note will sound a half step higher. Since there are twelve notes in an octave, the first note repeats itself at the 12th fret. As you get to know the fretboard, you'll discover it's important to know where your octaves are.

You can apply the note pattern that began on low E to other parts of the fretboard. For example, look at the note A on the top E string. Play the first six notes going up from A: A, A♯/B♭, B, C, C♯/D♭, D. Notice how that D note sounds the same as the D on the string next to the A you started on. You'll find this pattern works everywhere on the fretboard.

Also notice where octaves occur. For example, look at that same note A. You'll find its octave if you move two strings down and two frets toward the neck. This configuration works for many notes.

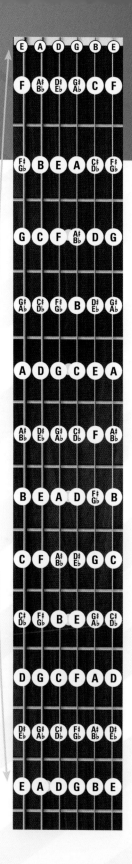

SCALES: THE BUILDING BLOCKS OF CHORDS

We'll avoid complicated music theory for the most part in this book. However, it is important to become familiar with a few fundamentals like scales. Simply put, scales are an ordered series of notes differing in pitch. They are the building blocks that help musicians compose and perform songs.

Let's start with the major scale. To our ears, it has a natural, sunny sound. This quality is caused by the scale's *intervals*. When we look at the major scale we see that there are half steps between notes three and four, and between seven and eight.

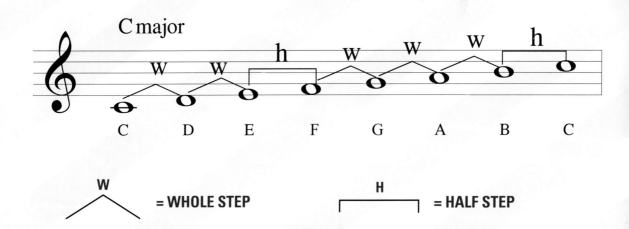

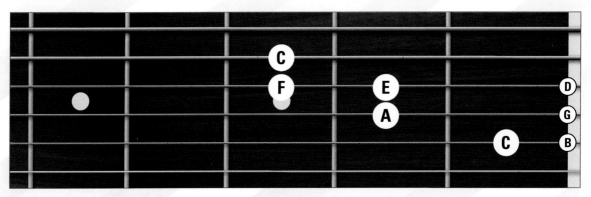

Notes of the C major scale on the fretboard

An interval is the distance between two notes. Intervals between notes vary as the scale moves upward. They may consist of whole or half steps. Intervals are a fundamental part of basic harmony and chord structure.

Now let's look at how you would play this scale on the fretboard. There are many ways to play this scale on guitar, but the lowest position is a good place to start. The numbers in the circles indicate which finger to use. A zero within the circle means the string is played open—with no finger on a fret. You'll begin with the lowest note. So the first note (C on the A string), will be played by the third finger. The second note is the open D string, the third note (E on the D string) will be played by the second finger, etc.

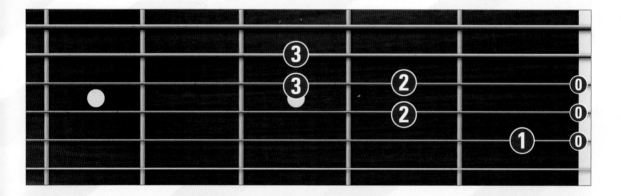

MUSICAL NOTES: PITCH = FREQUENCY

All musical notes have specific, set pitches. A pitch is essentially the same as the frequency of a sound. A frequency is simply the number of sound waves that moves past a point in one second. The greater the number of waves per second, the higher the frequency will be.

Let's look at another major scale. While the notes are different, the intervals remain the same. Note also, that in this scale there is a sharp that raises the F note a half step.

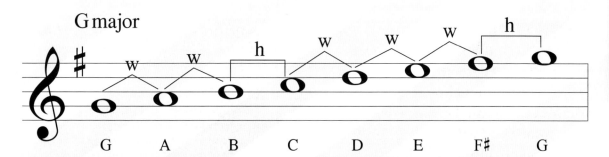

G major

G   A   B   C   D   E   F♯   G

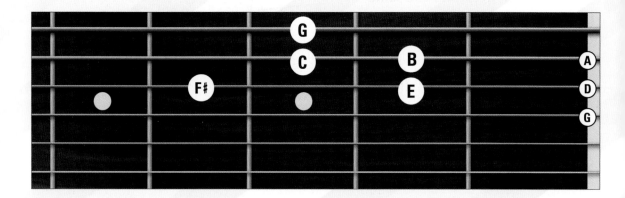

On the fretboard, begin with the G on the E string, using your third finger.

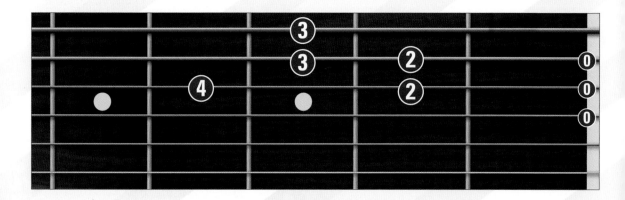

CHORDS

Like scales, chords can be played in a variety of positions on the fretboard. In this book, we'll keep it simple and learn first position chords. The more complex the music becomes, the more your hand will move around the fretboard. Often you'll have more than one finger on the same fret. As you progress, you can move on to other chord voicings.

Chords are made when you play two or more notes at the same time. The most common, a *triad*, is when three notes are combined. A triad is the superposition of two thirds. The notes are named the *root*, *third*, and *fifth*. This triad from the C major scale consists of C, E, and G.

THE TELECASTER

In the early 1950s, the first solid-body electric guitar was introduced commercially. The Telecaster is simple in design, featuring a one-piece body, a bolt-on neck, and two pickups controlled by a three-position selector. There is one volume and one tone control.

fifth
third
root

KEY SIGNATURES

The C and G major scales illustrate how scales are related to each other. If you divide the C major scale in half, you will notice that both the first half and the second half use the same configuration of half steps and whole steps—and that the two halves are separated by a whole step. Since the half step/whole step formula is the same for both halves of the scale, and since all major scales use the same formula, you can construct a new scale that begins with the second half of the C major scale. The example here shows that the resulting scale will be a G major scale.

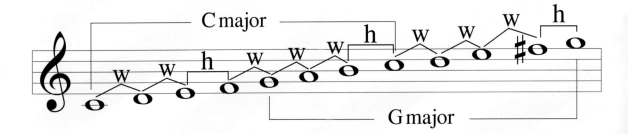

Unlike the C major scale, which has no sharps or flats, the G major scale must always have an F♯ to make it conform to the major-scale formula of half steps and whole steps. Since the key of G major always contains an F♯, this F♯ appears in the key signature of G major.

Let's try the same thing with the G major scale. The new scale starts on D. Once again we will have to add a sharp to make sure the scale conforms to the major scale formula of half steps and whole steps. As a result, the key signature for D major contains two sharps: F♯ and C♯.

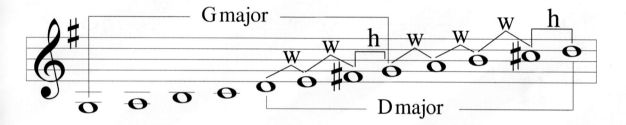

You can continue the pattern, starting at the fifth note of the last scale to start a new scale, and adding a sharp to maintain the major scale formula of half steps and whole steps. As you advance in music theory you may hear this referred to as the *circle of fifths*.

TABLATURE

In this book we will use an abbreviated form of music notation known as *tablature*. There are drawbacks to presenting music this way, however. In standard notation, rhythm is included in the note itself. The form of tablature you will be using uses slashes to represent rhythm. But this simplification will help you focus on mastering chords and progressions.

Let's get comfortable with tablature. The four measures below are identical to regular notation except for the slashes. These will stand for quarter notes. Most of the chord progressions in this book will keep the same quarter note strumming pattern.

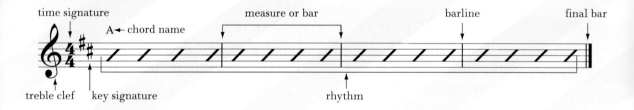

The $\frac{4}{4}$ time signature is the most common time in music. However, there are plenty of other time signatures to investigate. We'll try out the $\frac{3}{4}$ time signature later in the book.

KEEP TIME

People don't just hear music. They feel it too. As a musician, you need to develop a solid sense of rhythm. Rhythm comes from a Greek word that means "to flow." When you listen to music that doesn't have a solid rhythm, or flow, it can sound wrong or amateurish.

Using a timekeeping device while practicing is a great way to improve your sense of time and rhythm. A metronome—a kind of musical clock that will tick at the speed you set it to—was often used by musicians in the last century to develop this skill. You can still find metronomes, but today it's easier to just download a timekeeping or metronome app to a digital device like a smartphone.

CHORDS: YOUR MUSICAL TOOLBOX

There are many chord types, but all of them are based on scales. So once you learn a scale, you should be able to form chords based on its notes. The notes of a chord may be played simultaneously or in quick succession (in which case the chord is called an *arpeggio*). Chords can be strummed by string instruments, played on keyboards, or voiced by several instruments simultaneously.

In this book we'll cover the most common, frequently used chords played on the guitar. We'll start with the C, D, G, and F major chords. With just these four chords you can play a wealth of songs. In fact, these four chords will allow you to play *thousands* of songs.

You may be surprised to learn that chords have personalities. When you listen to a song and identify it with a mood—sad, nostalgic, angry, or blissful—you are reacting to the power of the song's chords. We'll look at this aspect of chord types too. Once you have a basic understanding of how a chord type can change the feeling of a song, you'll be able to pick the right one out of your chord toolbox for whatever mood the chord progression needs.

IN THE EAR OF
THE BEHOLDER

If you want to start an argument between two songwriters, ask them what gives chords their different moods. The debate has been raging for a long time, but here are a few common opinions:

- Chords are simply pitch combinations that we have heard since childhood and have been conditioned to associate with different emotions. In other words, it's cultural.

- Wrong—it's biological! Our ears naturally hear some intervals within chords as consonant (harmonious or settled) and others as dissonant. We assign moods to chords based on their relative consonance/dissonance.

- It depends on the company a chord keeps. A single minor chord in a progression of major chords may be very soothing. Group that chord with other minor chords and it may sound melancholy.

MAJOR CHORDS

Major chords are often described in positive terms like happy, upbeat, open, and simple. These are the workhorses of the chord stable and the most common and important chords you will learn.

THE **C MAJOR** CHORD

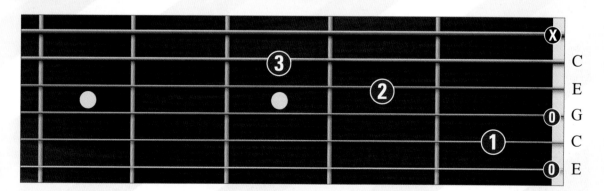

Look at the fretboard diagram and use the picture to help position your fingers. Now try *strumming*—running your pick over the five strings used in this chord. Note the  on the top string. This means the string is not played.

If you hear any buzzing while you strum, you probably aren't pressing down hard enough on one of the strings. Or you may be blocking one of the open strings. Check your finger positions and practice getting a good, clear tone before moving on to the next page.

START WITH STRUMMING

Strumming downward is called a
downstroke. Remember to make sure your
pick is at a ninety degree angle to the
strings. On the staff below, a downstroke
is indicated with this symbol: ⊓ . The
chord name is given above the staff. Play
these four bars until you get comfortable
with the downstroke technique.

Now let's try playing the same C chord using
upstrokes. Strum upward from the high E
(thinnest string, closest to the floor) to the C
you're holding down with your ring finger.
On the staff below, an upstroke is indicated
with this symbol: V

Now try playing with up- and downstrokes combined.

THE LES PAUL

First produced in 1952, this solid-body electric guitar has remained virtually unchanged for over half a century. Its thick, heavy body gives it a thick tone with notable sustain.

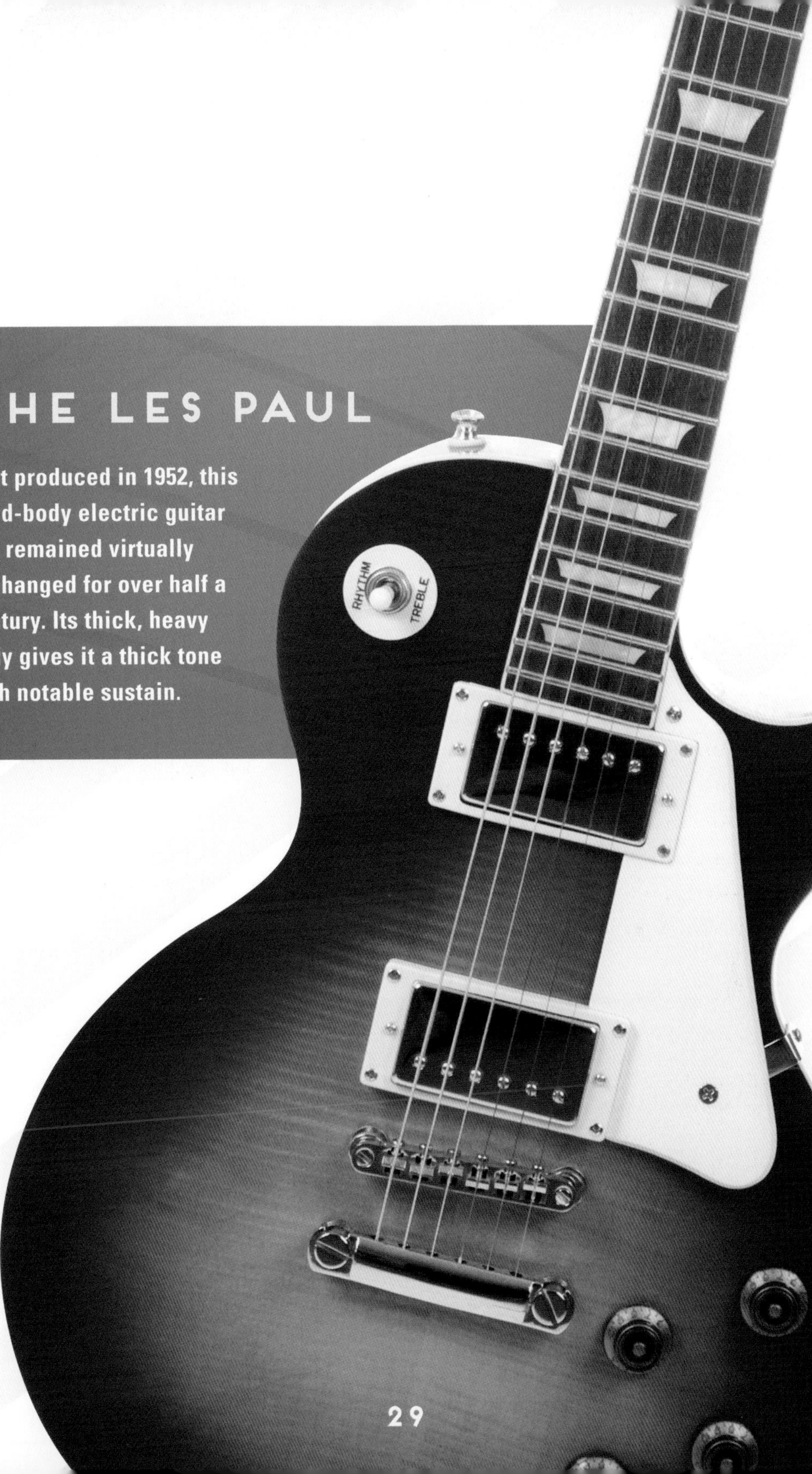

RHYTHM

TREBLE

Here's the D major scale in the lowest position. As with all the other major scales, there are many ways to play this scale on your fretboard. Remember that the numbers indicate finger positions. Begin on the open D string.

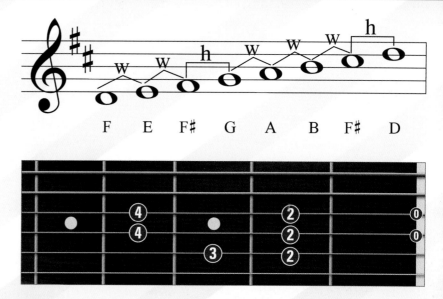

F   E   F♯   G   A   B   F♯   D

THE **D MAJOR** CHORD

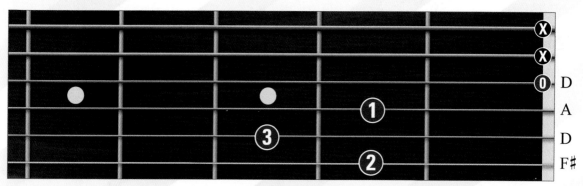

Look at the fretboard diagram and use the picture to help position your fingers. Note that the top two strings are not played.

Let's learn one more chord and then add it to our first chord progression. The G major chord is absolutely essential, no matter what style of music you play. This big, full-sounding chord uses all six strings on the guitar.

THE **G MAJOR** CHORD

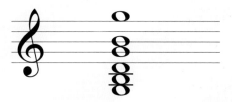

IT'S TIME TO PLAY

Try out this chord progression: two bars of C, then two bars of G, alternating. Follow the downstroke/upstroke symbols and play as slowly as you need to until your playing sounds smooth and rhythmic.

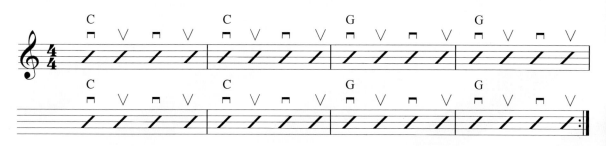

Moving from C to G can be a little tricky using the fingering we learned, so try out this alternate fingering for the G chord. You may find it works better for you.

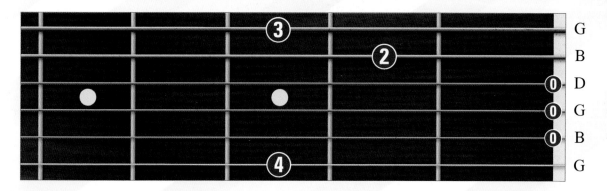

THINK AHEAD

When you're playing a chord progression, try visualizing what you're going to play beforehand. This will help you get your fingers ready to move to new positions on the fretboard.

ADD A BIT MORE

Now let's add the D major chord to this progression.

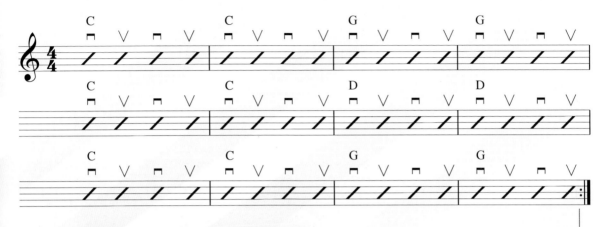

Did you notice the two bars preceded by two dots? This indicates that the progression is to be repeated once from the beginning.

IT'S IN THE WRIST

Your wrist needs to stay relaxed and flexible while you're strumming. Make sure it's not rigid. Downward and upward movements should travel about the same distance in order to keep a smooth rhythm.

Here's the A major scale in its lowest position. Another sharp has been added to the scale, for a total of three: C#, F#, G#. Begin on the open A string.

Now let's learn another important chord.

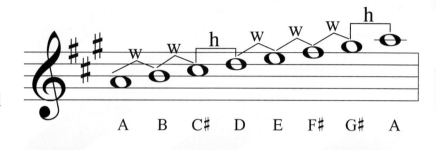

A   B   C#   D   E   F#   G#   A

THE **A MAJOR** CHORD

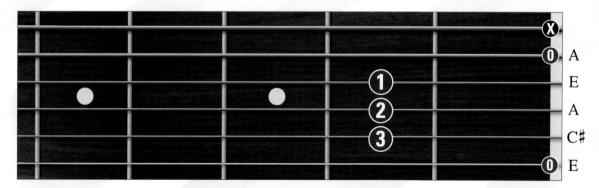

PUT IT TOGETHER

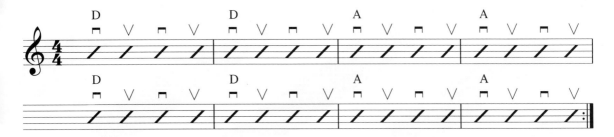

Now try the three-chord progression below. It almost sounds like a song, doesn't it?

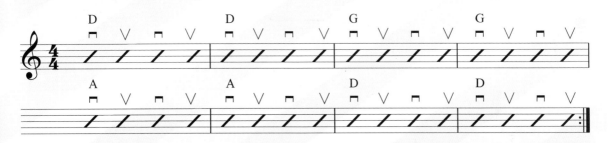

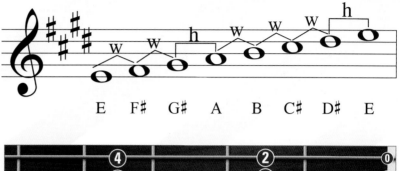

E   F#   G#   A   B   C#   D#   E

Here's the E major scale in its lowest position. Another sharp has been added to the scale, for a total of four: C#, D#, F#, G#.

THE **E MAJOR** CHORD

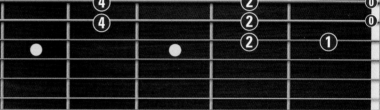

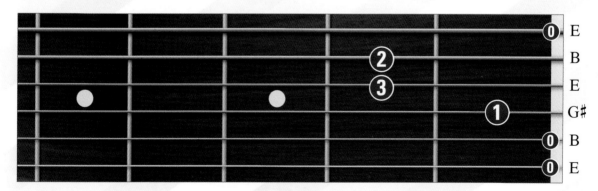

This versatile chord has a big, rich sound when all six strings are strummed. The first position E chord was an essential part of the early blues and sixties folk rock.

SMOOTH OUT YOUR TRANSITIONS

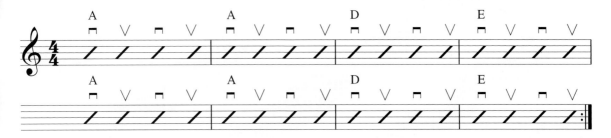

Now try this progression, incorporating the E, A, D, and G chords.

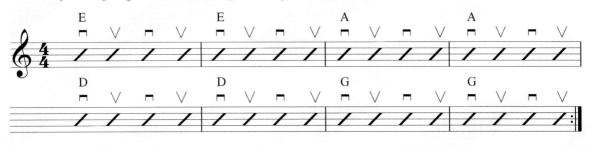

The 12-string guitar produces a rich, ringing sound. Each pair of strings is set closely together so that one finger can hold down both strings at the same time. These paired strings are tuned differently, with one string being tuned an entire octave higher than the other. The result, when chords are strummed, is a full, shimmering effect.

LET'S PUT IT ALL TOGETHER

Remember to think about upcoming chord changes as you play this—especially since things get a little tricky in the ninth and tenth bars. There are two chords in each of those measures, on the first and third beats, so be prepared! Play along slowly until your changes sound smooth. Then try speeding up the tempo.

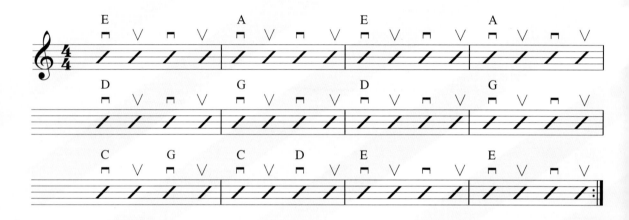

So far, you've been strumming chords in quarter note rhythms. When you feel ready, try using eighth notes. As you become more competent, you will want to *syncopate* (shift, divide, or otherwise accent the beat differently) your strumming patterns to make them more complex and interesting.

THE **F MAJOR** CHORD

F
A
C
F

You now know the most important major chords a beginner should know. However, there are other major chords beyond the ones used in this book. They are B, C♯/D♭, D♯/E♭, F♯/G♭, G♯/A♭, and A♯/B♭. You'll get to know these as you become a more advanced player.

Let's play one more major chord progression using the chord you just learned.

You have now learned some major chords and tried them out in a few simple chord progressions. Knowing these chords will serve you well down the road. They appear in countless chord progressions in songs of every style and genre.

The chords C♯/D♭, D♯/E♭, F♯/G♭, G♯/A♭, and A♯/B♭ can be denoted in two ways—flat or sharp—depending on the musical context, or key signature. But the notes (and finger positions) are exactly the same. (We present both names in the upcoming chord sections for your reference.)

Each chord section presents chords in their first position, and provides three alternate voicings. As you become more comfortable with the fretboard, you'll want to explore these alternates. They allow you to make easier transitions from one chord to another, extend pitch range, and broaden your tonal palette.

One great thing about the fretboard is that once you know a voicing for one chord (for example, D Major) you can usually use that finger position for the other eleven chords. For example:

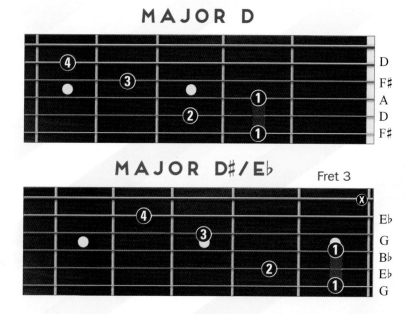

MAJOR D

D
F♯
A
D
F♯

MAJOR D♯/E♭   Fret 3

E♭
G
B♭
E♭
G

In this case you are simply sliding your fingers up one fret to make the same major chord, which now becomes D♯/E♭. Get in the habit of remembering these finger positions, or chord shapes as they're sometimes called. It will help to expand your chord-playing repertoire and allow you to move between chord voicings on the fly.

C MAJOR

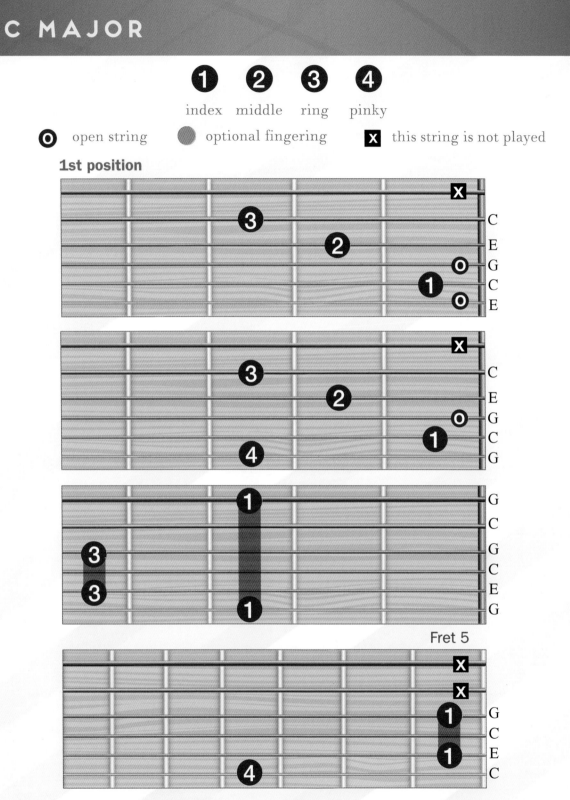

C# (D♭) MAJOR

1st position

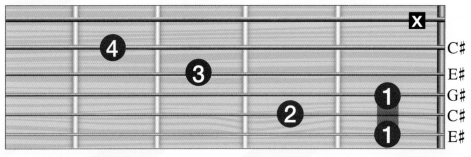

C#
E#
G#
C#
E#

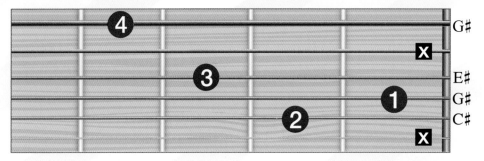

G#

E#
G#
C#

Fret 4

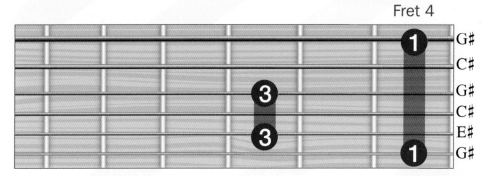

G#
C#
G#
C#
E#
G#

Fret 6

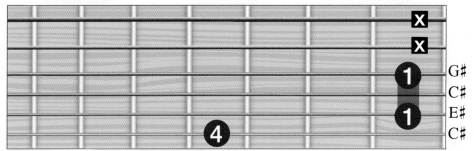

G#
C#
E#
C#

42

1st position

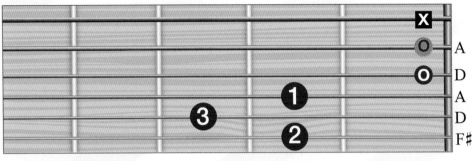

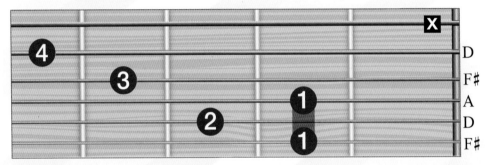

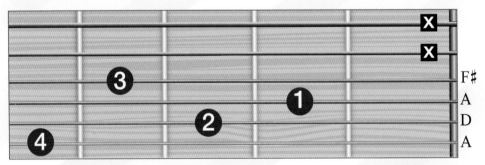

Fret 5

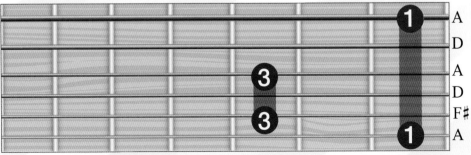

(D♯) E♭ MAJOR

1st position

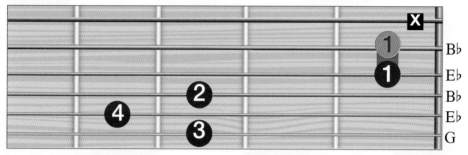

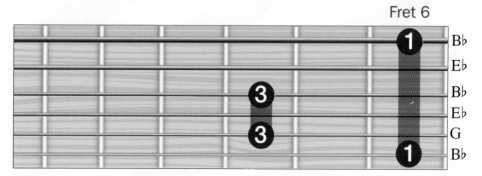

Fret 3

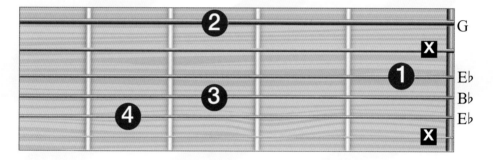

Fret 6

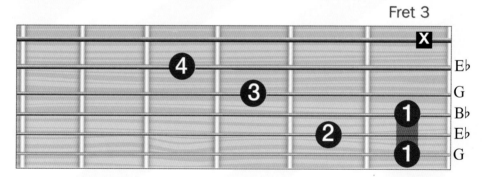

E MAJOR

1st position

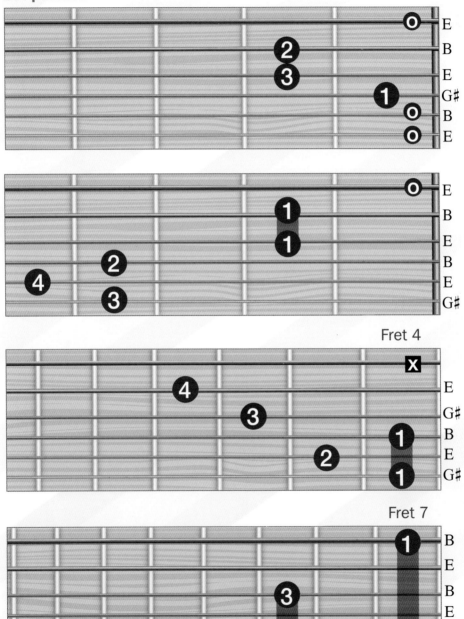

F MAJOR

1st position

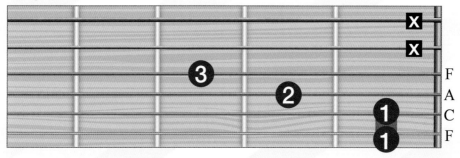

F
A
C
F

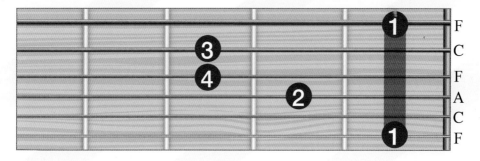

F
C
F
A
C
F

Fret 5

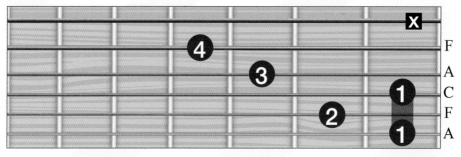

F
A
C
F
A

Fret 8

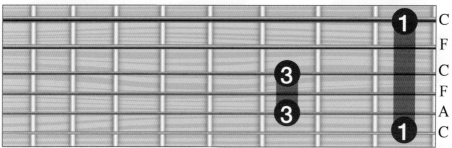

C
F
C
F
A
C

F♯ (G♭) MAJOR

1st position

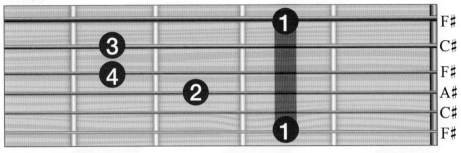

F♯
C♯
F♯
A♯
C♯
F♯

Fret 4

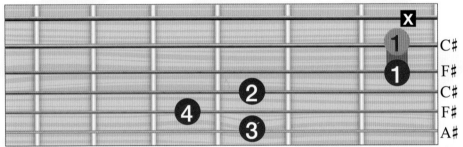

C♯
F♯
C♯
F♯
A♯

Fret 6

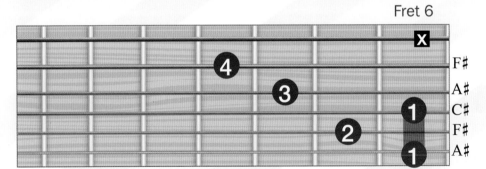

F♯
A♯
C♯
F♯
A♯

Fret 9

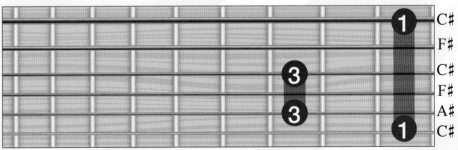

C♯
F♯
C♯
F♯
A♯
C♯

G MAJOR

1st position

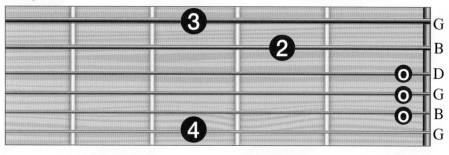

Fret 3

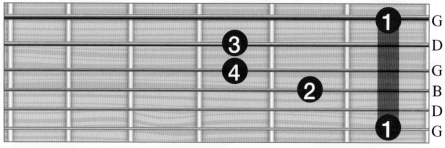

Fret 5

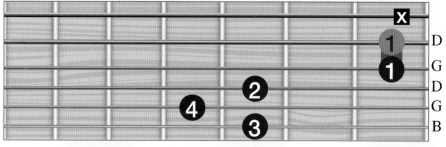

Fret 7

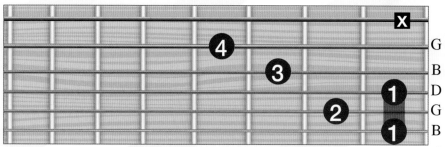

1st position

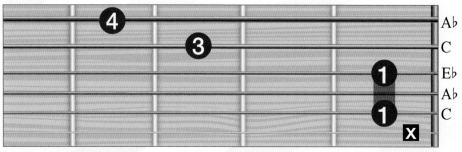

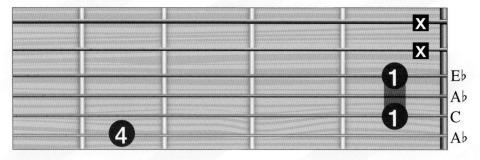

Fret 4

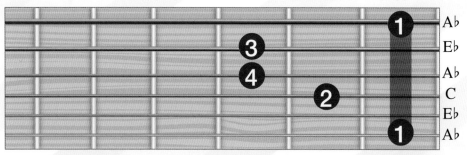

Fret 6

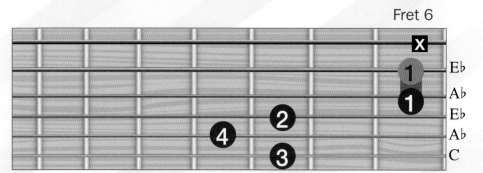

1st position

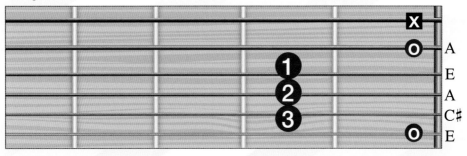

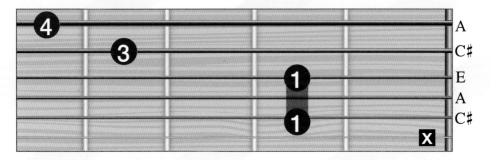

Fret 5

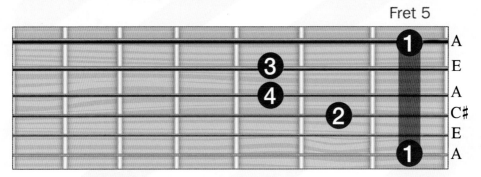

Fret 7

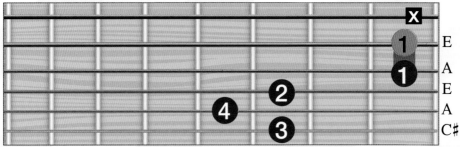

(A♯) B♭ MAJOR

1st position

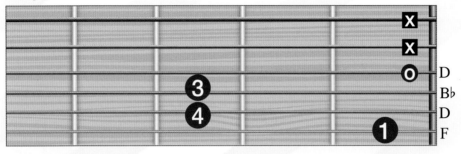

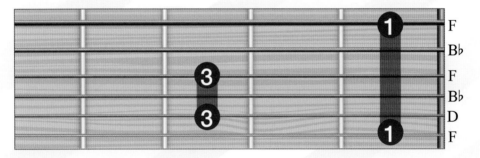

Fret 3

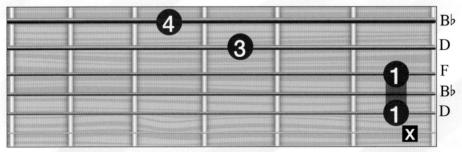

Fret 6

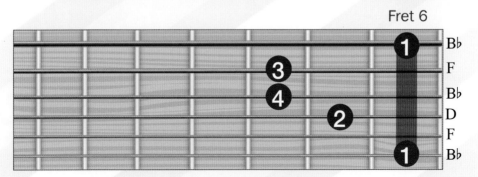

1st position

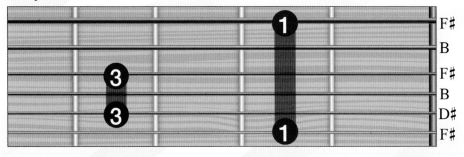

F#
B
F#
B
D#
F#

Fret 4

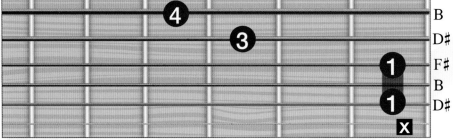

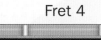

B
D#
F#
B
D#

Fret 7

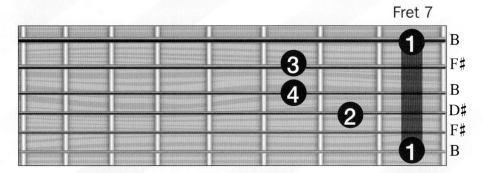

B
F#
B
D#
F#
B

Fret 9

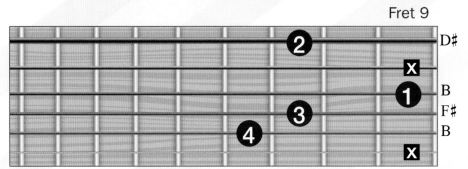

D#
B
F#
B

MINOR CHORDS

If major chords suggest sunny days and smooth sailing, then minor chords are the bringers of gloom and rain—or at least clouds on the horizon. Minor chords are usually perceived as somber, reflective, and serious. However, you will learn in the coming chord progressions that when you mix major and minor chords, the results are much more interesting than simply going from happy to sad.

You'll probably find that the three most common minor scales you use are the *natural*, *harmonic*, and *melodic* scales. All major scales have corresponding relative minor scales. The relative minor scale can be determined by starting on the sixth step of any major scale. For example, start on the sixth step of a C scale and play each major scale note in succession (ABCDEFG) to create an A minor scale. Therefore A minor is the relative minor of C major. This scale is said to be *natural* because it follows the major-scale formula without altering the key signature.

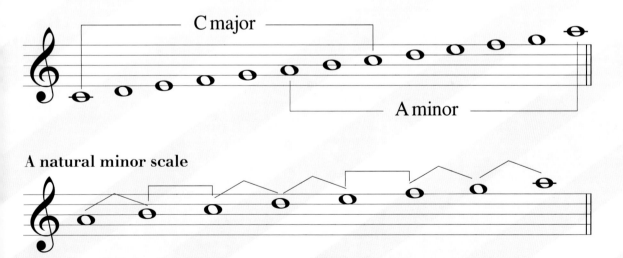

We won't use the other minor scales in this book, but they're good to know—you'll meet them again down the road as an advanced player. The harmonic minor scale has half steps between notes two and three, five and six, and seven and eight. Notice that the distance between notes six and seven is a *minor third* (three half steps).

A harmonic minor scale

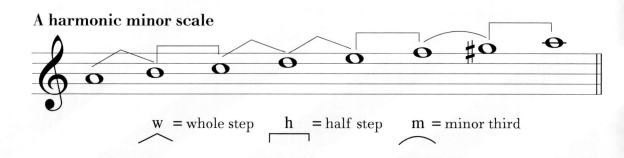

w = whole step   h = half step   m = minor third

The melodic minor scale's ascending order finds half steps between two and three and between seven and eight. Unlike any of the other scales that have been discussed so far, melodic minor scales have a different descending order. The descending order has half steps between notes six and five and between three and two—with a whole step between notes eight and seven.

A melodic minor scale (ascending)

A melodic minor scale (descending)

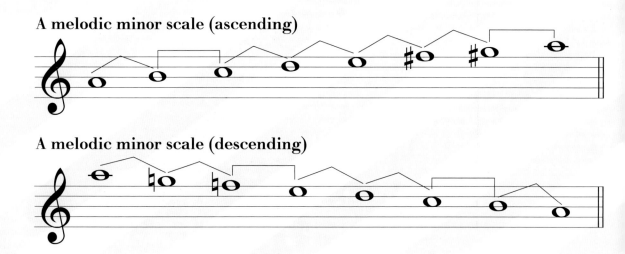

The key of E minor is the relative minor to the key of G. So an E minor scale will start on E and have one sharp.

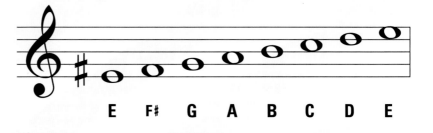

E F# G A B C D E

THE E MINOR CHORD

	0	E
2		B
3		E
	0	G
	0	B
	0	E

The E minor (Em) chord sounds very different than the chords you've learned so far. You'll hear this dark quality in all the minor chords.

Try a simple chord progression from E major to E minor.

Now let's alternate E minor with G major. Notice how mixing major and minor chords affects the mood of the progression.

CHORD FINGERING REVIEW

E MAJOR CHORD

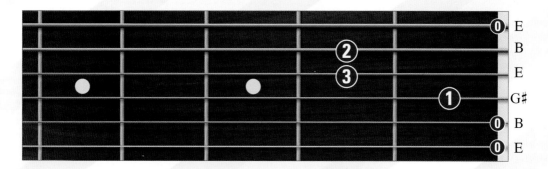

G MAJOR CHORD

THE POWER OF THE MINOR CHORD

Now let's integrate E minor into a longer chord progression. Notice how this chord alters the mood.

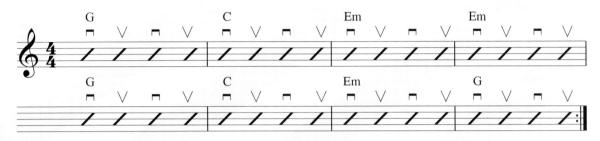

THE STRATOCASTER

A top-seller since 1954, the iconic Stratocaster is simply designed but amazingly versatile in tone. Its three single coil pickups provide guitarists with a broad tonal palette.

THE A MINOR CHORD

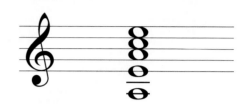

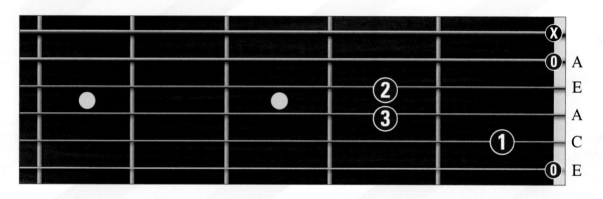

The A minor chord is a favorite of folk musicians. When you pair it with the E minor chord, the result is a distinctly dark and moody feeling.

Now try the A minor chord with a few major chords.

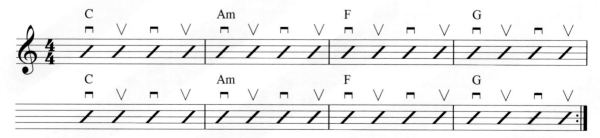

MAJOR-MINOR MIX

Try these two progressions using both of the minor chords you've learned. Notice how much atmosphere they bring to the sequence.

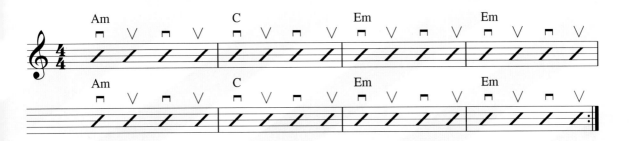

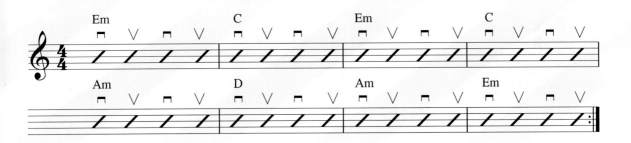

THE **D MINOR** CHORD

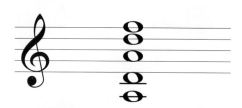

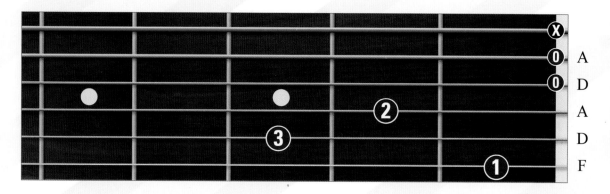

Most of the chords you have learned have had the root note on the lowest string of those chords. The D minor chord can be played with just four strings—allowing the lowest string to be a D—but the most common usage is with an open A as the lowest note.

Now let's try a progression using all minor chords.

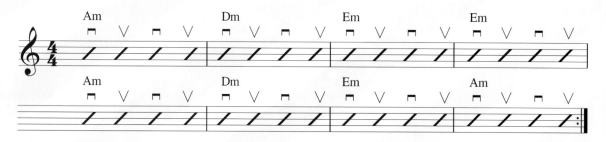

PUTTING IT ALL TOGETHER

You've come a long way! You now know enough chords to play a rich, songlike chord progression. Remember to think ahead to the next chord fingering as you play.

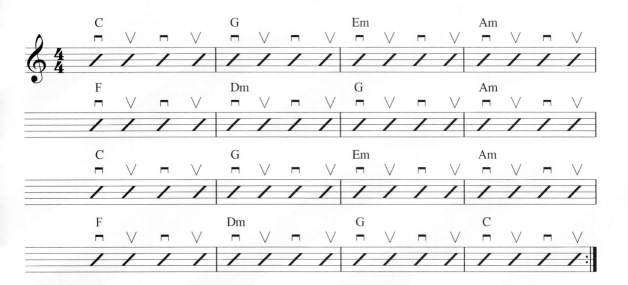

GUITAR CASE

You need one. Soft cases may prevent a few scratches, but to truly protect your guitar from injury, you should invest in a hard plastic or fiberglass case.

BEYOND $\frac{4}{4}$

You already know $\frac{4}{4}$. Now let's take a more in-depth look at time signatures. The beat is the pulse of a musical composition. Time signatures regulate that pulse. The time signature provides two important pieces of rhythmic information: How many beats does a measure get, and how long do those beats last?

A time signature consists of two numbers. The top number determines how many beats there will be in a measure. The bottom number indicates the duration of each beat.

> **Top number** = number of beats in a measure
>
> **Bottom number** = the value of one beat

> **If the bottom number is:**
>
> **1** = the whole note receives one beat
>
> **2** = the half note receives one beat
>
> **4** = the quarter note receives one beat
>
> **8** = the eighth note receives one beat
>
> **16** = the sixteenth note receives one beat

THE $\frac{3}{4}$ TIME SIGNATURE

$\frac{3}{4}$ is often called waltz time. It has been the basis for many dance compositions. Simply subtract a beat from $\frac{4}{4}$ and you have $\frac{3}{4}$. When you're playing music in $\frac{3}{4}$ and other more unusual time signatures, it may be helpful to mentally count out the number of beats in your head.

TRY IT IN THREE

These progressions give you a sense of just how much you can do when mixing majors and minors. Note that the progression on the next page is in $\frac{3}{4}$.

Hold the last note.

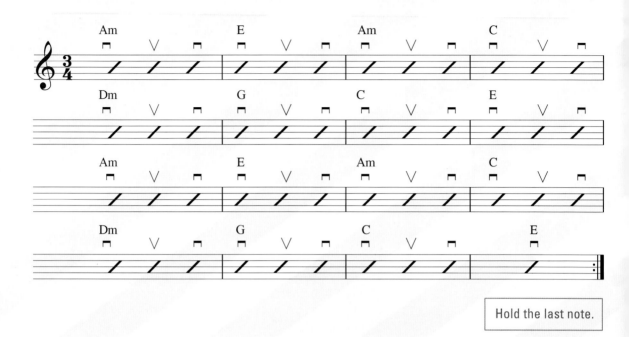

Hold the last note.

Experiment with your down- and upstrokes in the $\frac{3}{4}$ time signature. You may find a pattern that is easier or better-sounding than this one.

People who make guitars are called *luthiers*. The word is related to the word "lute."

1st position

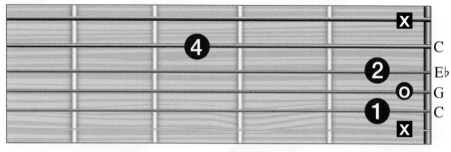

Fret 3

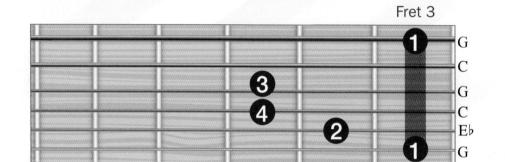

Fret 4

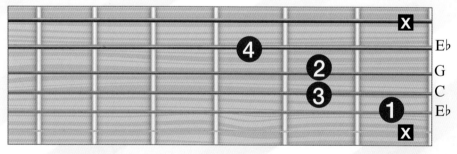

Fret 5

C# (Db) MINOR

1st position

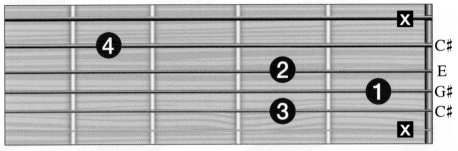

C#
E
G#
C#

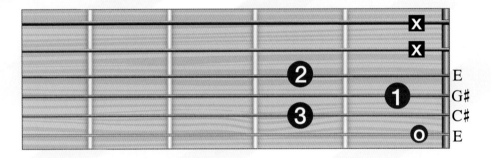

E
G#
C#
E

Fret 4

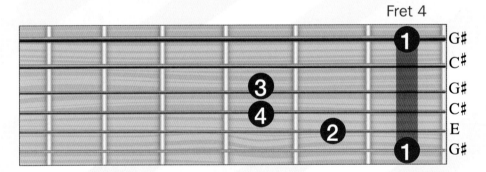

G#
C#
G#
C#
E
G#

Fret 6

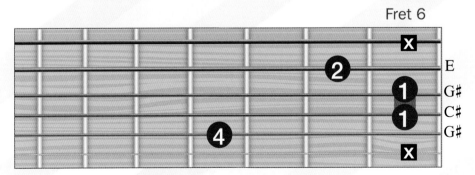

E
G#
C#
G#

66

D MINOR

1st position

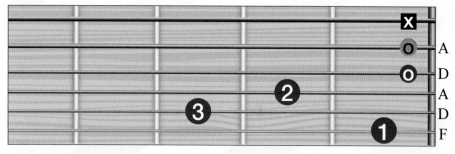

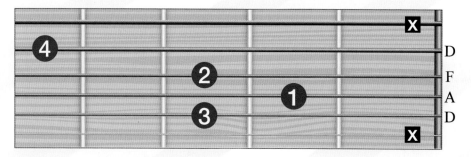

Fret 5

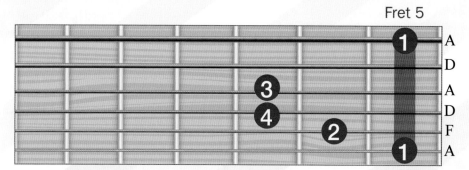

Fret 7

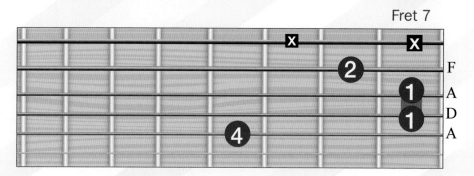

(D♯) E♭ MINOR

1st position

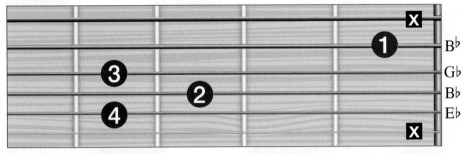

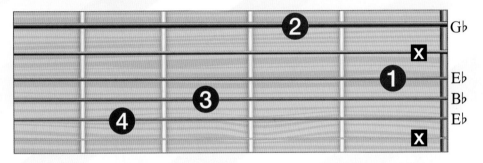

Fret 6

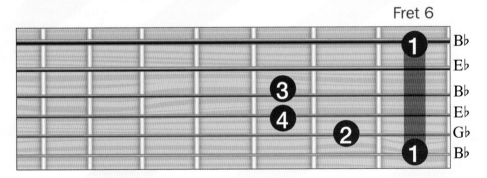

Fret 8

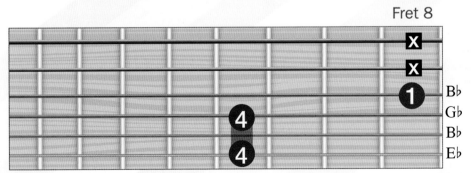

E MINOR

1st position

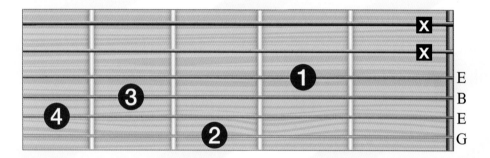

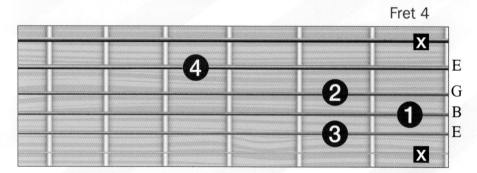

Fret 4

Fret 7

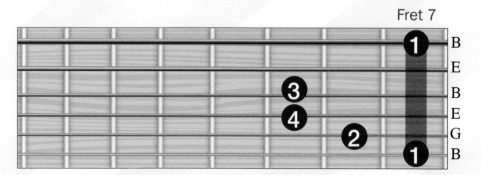

F MINOR

1st position

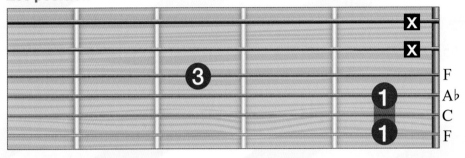

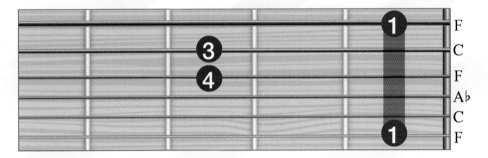

Fret 4

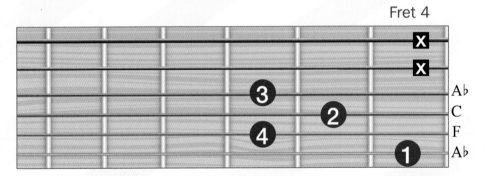

Fret 5

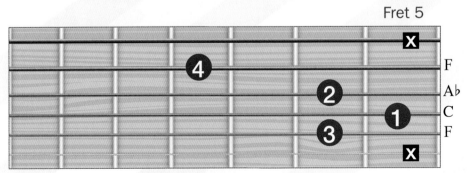

F♯ (G♭) MINOR

1st position

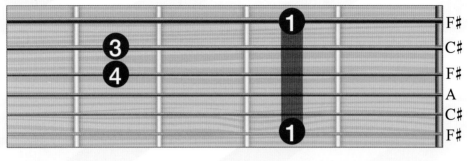

F♯
C♯
F♯
A
C♯
F♯

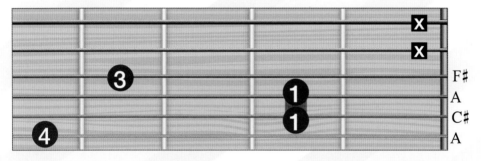

X
X
F♯
A
C♯
A

Fret 4

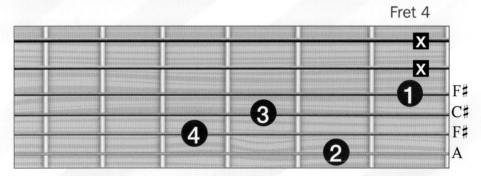

X
X
F♯
C♯
F♯
A

Fret 6

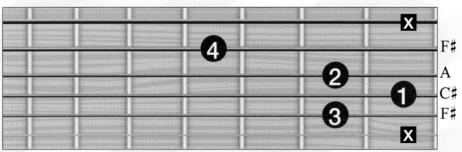

X
F♯
A
C♯
F♯
X

G MINOR

1st position

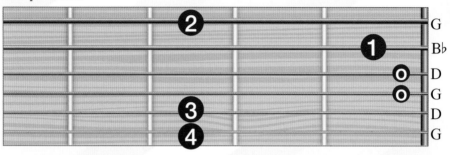

Fret 3

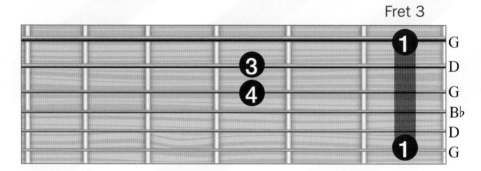

Fret 3

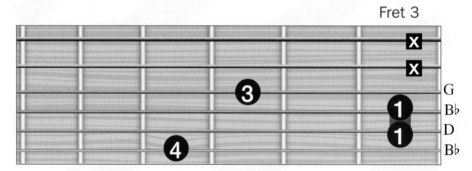

Fret 5

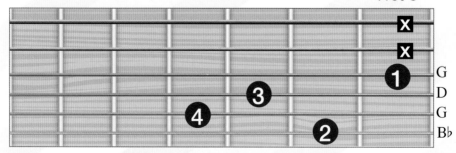

1st position

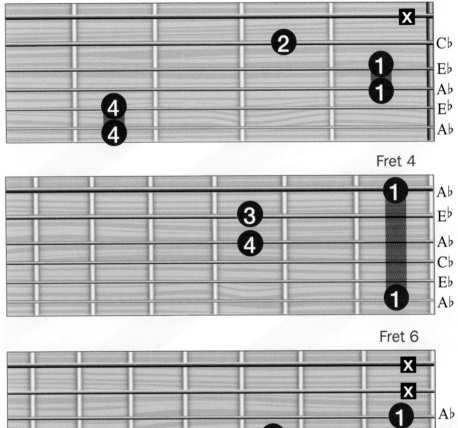

Fret 4

Fret 6

Fret 8

1st position

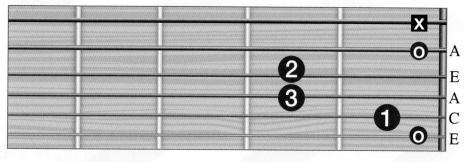

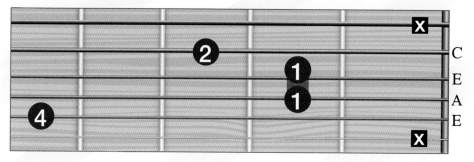

Fret 5

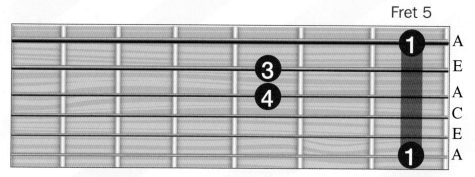

Fret 7

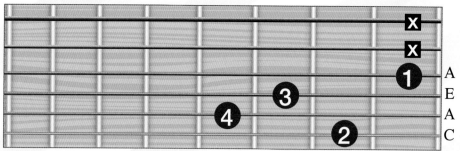

(A♯) B♭ MINOR

1st position

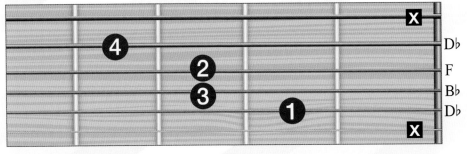

D♭
F
B♭
D♭

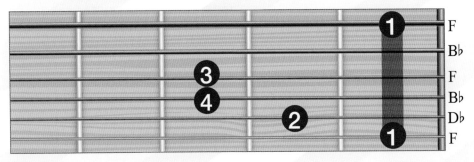

Fret 3

F
B♭
F
B♭
D♭
F

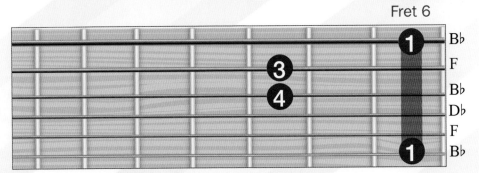

Fret 6

F
D♭
F
B♭

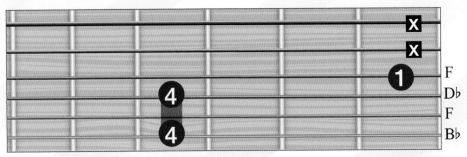

B♭
F
B♭
D♭
F
B♭

75

1st position

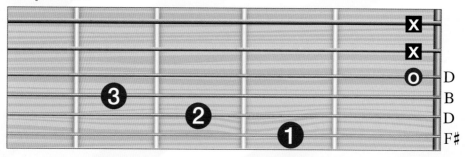

D
B
D
F#

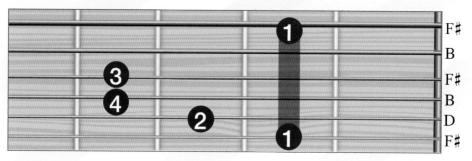

F#
B
F#
B
D
F#

Fret 3

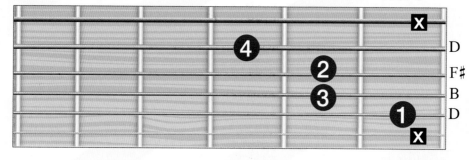

D
F#
B
D

Fret 7

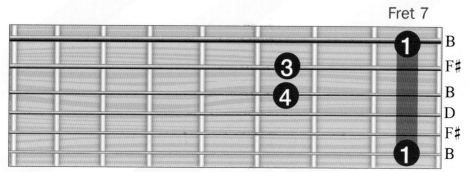

B
F#
B
D
F#
B

DOMINANT SEVENTH CHORDS

If a chord progression is a storyline, then dominant sevenths show up when the plot gets complicated. These chords have the vigor of major chords, while being more complex and unresolved. They're great to throw into the mix when the progression needs some adventurous tension.

THE A DOMINANT SEVENTH CHORD

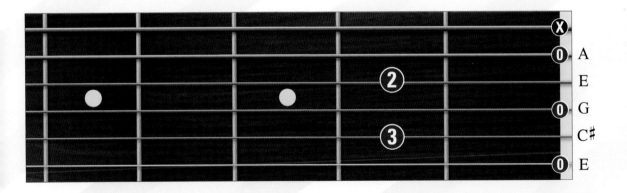

The A7 chord, like many dominant sevenths in the open position, is essentially its major chord equivalent with slightly different fingering.

THE **D** DOMINANT SEVENTH CHORD

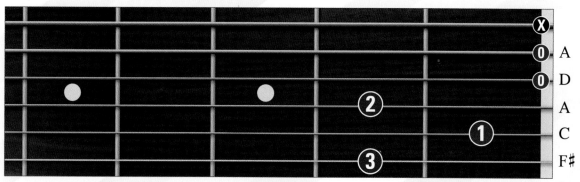

X
0 — A
0 — D
② — A
① — C
③ — F#

THE **E** DOMINANT SEVENTH CHORD

0 — E
② — B
0 — D
① — G#
0 — B
0 — E

Let's compare some major chords to dominant seventh equivalents. The first progression features the major chords A, D, E, and A. The second progression is played with the dominant equivalent of those chords.

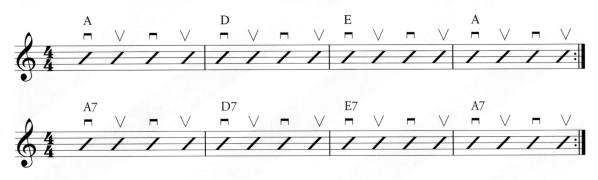

Now let's mix together the three chord types you've learned: major, minor, and dominant, using the same A/D/E/A sequence.

Blues guitarists use dominant sevenths like salt and pepper! If you want to develop a blues style, then you'll want to learn how to play this chord in every key.

THE G DOMINANT SEVENTH CHORD

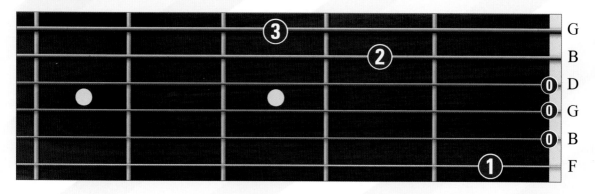

To get a sense of how the dominant seventh alters the mood of a progression, try swapping out the G7 in this progression for a regular G major.

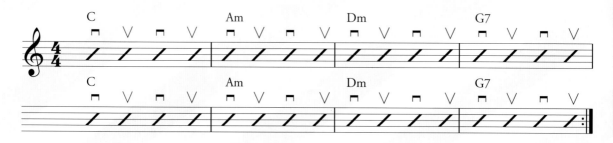

THE C DOMINANT SEVENTH CHORD

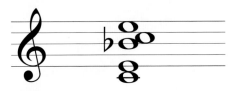

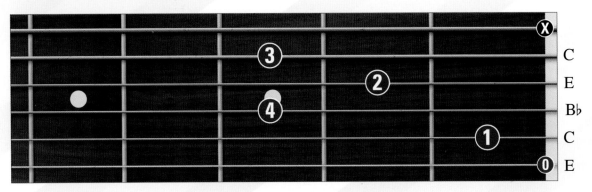

C
E
B♭
C
E

This C7 is another easy chord to play. Just make the regular C chord and place your fourth finger on the third fret of the third string.

Try the C7 and the G7 together in this progression.

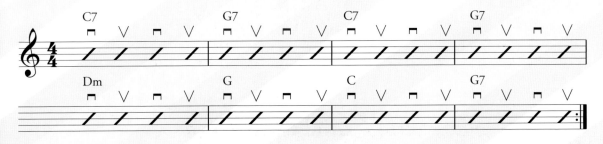

This progression is a little tricky. Some bars contain two chords, so it may take you a while to master all the finger work. Start out slowly, thinking ahead to the next chord.

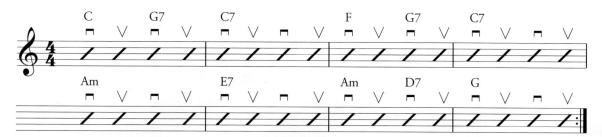

THE ES-335

The ES-335 was first manufactured in 1958. An electric guitar with a hollow body, this semi-acoustic instrument provides a great palette of sounds, from warm and mellow jazzy tones to bright, soaring leads. A solid block of wood beneath the pickups reduces feedback problems associated with semi-acoustic guitars.

C DOMINANT SEVENTH

1st position

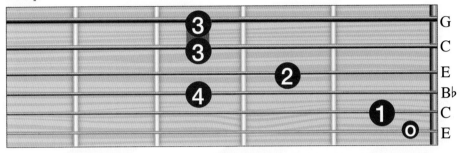

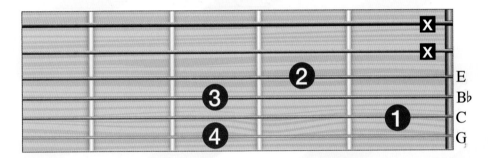

Fret 3

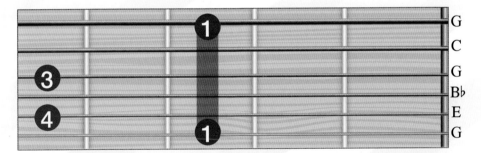

1st position

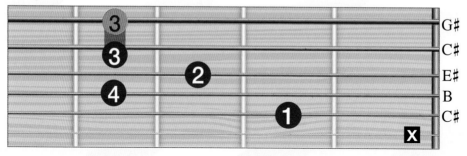

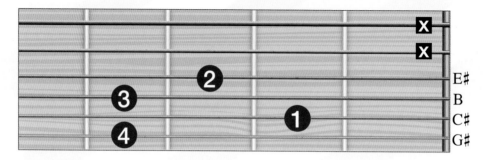

Fret 4

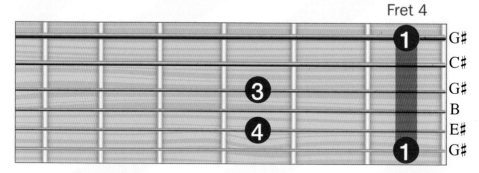

Fret 4

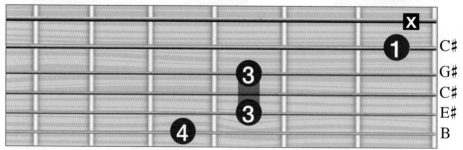

1st position

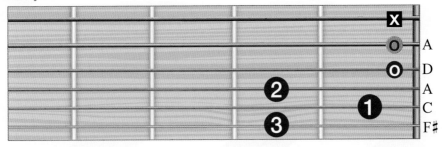

X
A
D
② A
① C
③ F#

Fret 3

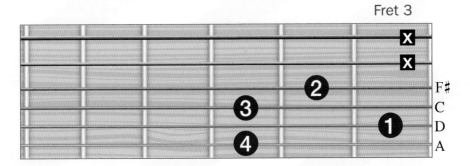

X
X
② F#
③ C
① D
④ A

Fret 5

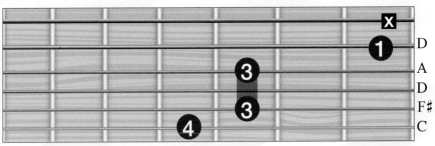

X
① D
③ A
D
③ F#
④ C

Fret 5

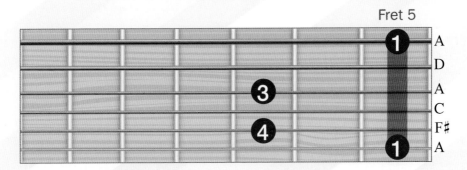

① A
D
③ A
C
④ F#
① A

1st position

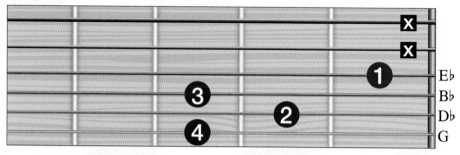

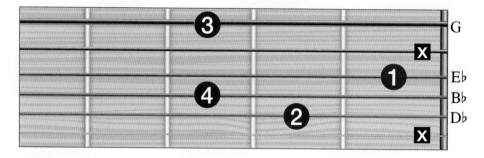

Fret 4

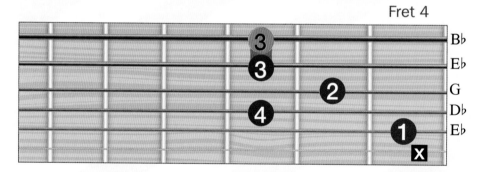

Fret 6

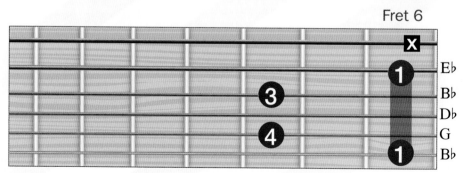

1st position

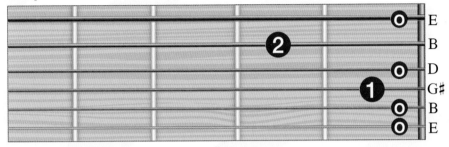

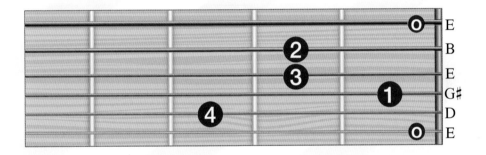

Fret 5

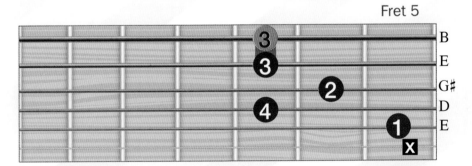

Fret 7

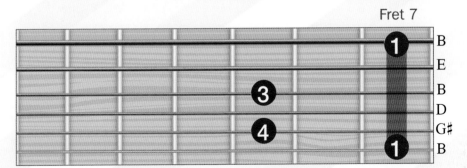

F DOMINANT SEVENTH

1st position

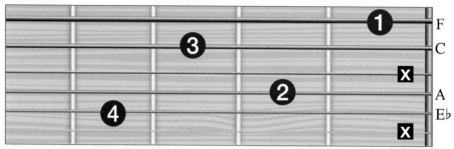

F
C
X
A
E♭
X

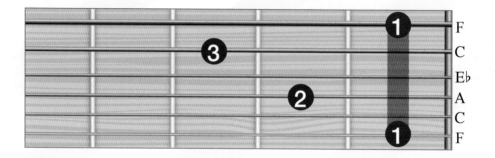

F
C
E♭
A
C
F

Fret 3

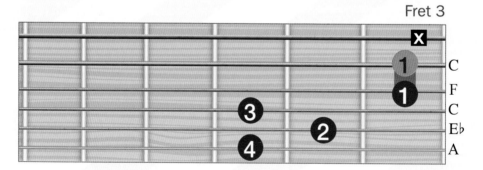

X
C
F
C
E♭
A

Fret 6

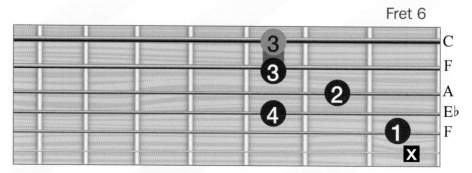

C
F
A
E♭
F
X

1st position

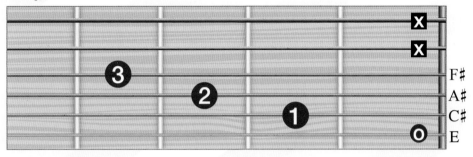

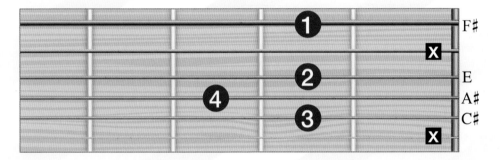

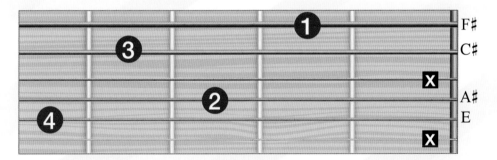

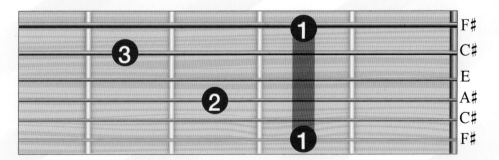

1st position

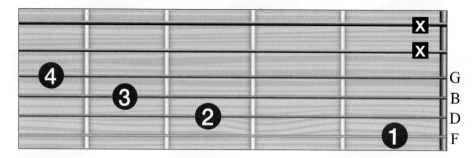

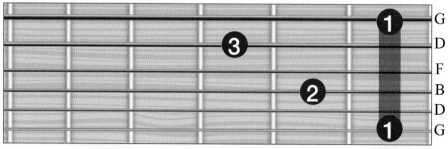

Fret 3

Fret 5

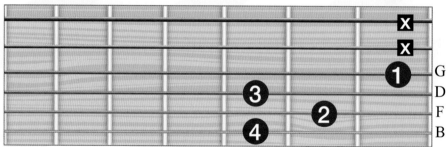

(G#) A♭ DOMINANT SEVENTH

1st position

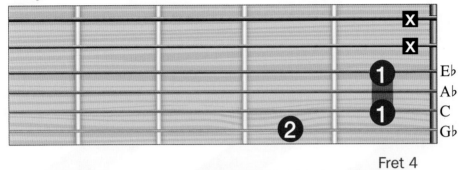

Fret 4

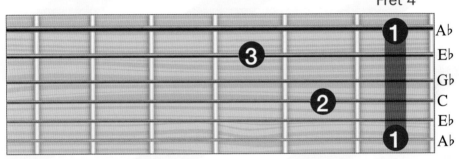

Fret 4

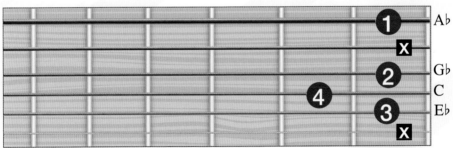

Fret 6

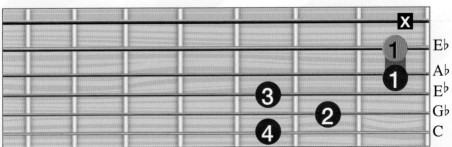

1st position

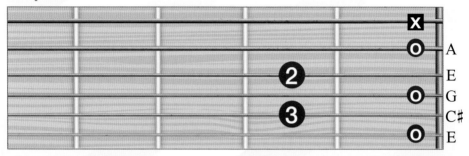

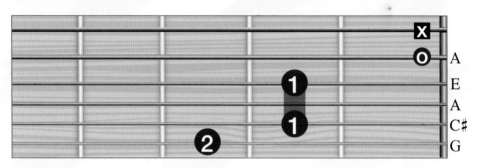

Fret 5

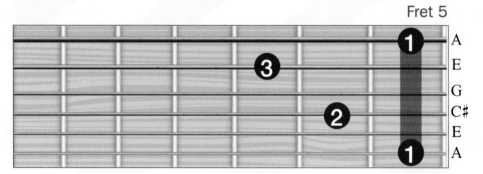

Fret 7

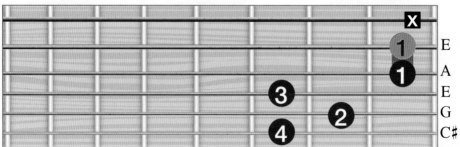

1st position

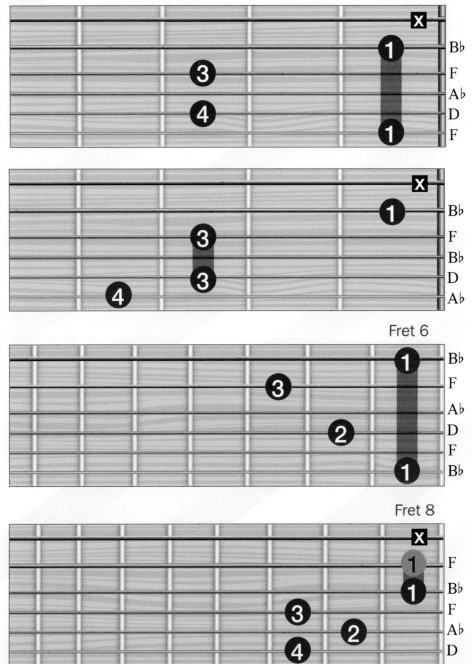

1st position

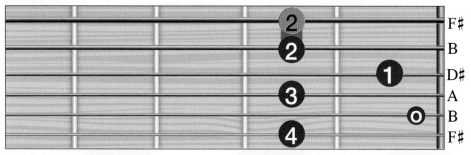

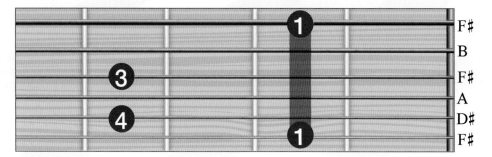

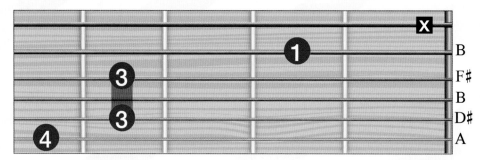

Fret 7

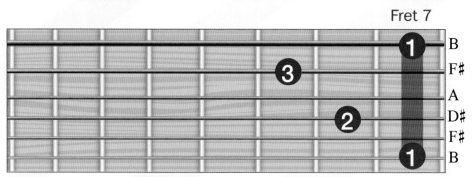

MAJOR SEVENTH CHORDS

Major seventh chords have a distinct personality that you will come to recognize as you grow familiar with them. These laid-back cousins of the major chords sound a bit contemplative, or even dreamy. However you choose to describe them, they offer lots of atmosphere and ambience to give color and nuance to a chord progression. You'll especially hear them in some jazz styles and pop ballads.

THE A MAJOR SEVENTH CHORD

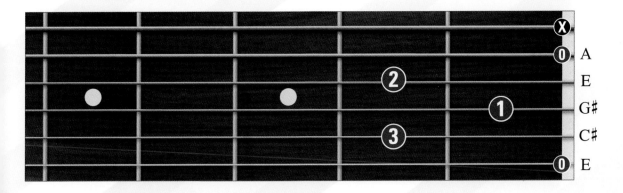

Play the A major and A major seventh chords side by side.
Listen to the difference that a single note makes.

THE C MAJOR SEVENTH CHORD

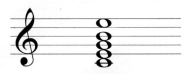

C
E
G
B
E

THE D MAJOR SEVENTH CHORD

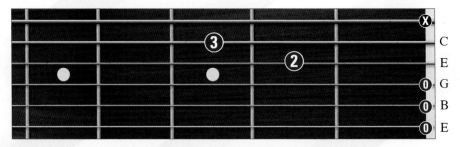

D
A
C#
F#

Let's put these three new chords together in a progression.

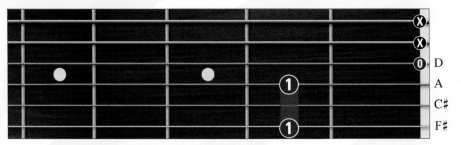

| Amaj7 | Cmaj7 | Amaj7 | Cmaj7 |

| Dmaj7 | Cmaj7 | Amaj7 | Cmaj7 |

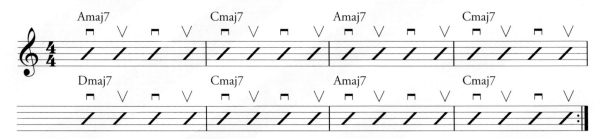

THE F MAJOR SEVENTH CHORD

As you may have noticed with the C major seventh, you can make an F major seventh by starting with its major chord equivalent. But instead of barring the first two strings with your first finger, just place your first finger on the second string at the first fret. Make sure the high E rings out and is not muted by the first finger.

Now play Fmaj7 together with Cmaj7.

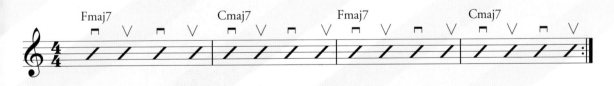

MIX IN SOME MAJOR SEVENTHS

This progression contains a minor chord you haven't played with other chords yet. Get comfortable with F minor first before tackling these chord changes.

Note how the phrasing makes it necessary to carry over the final chord into the thirteenth bar. Play that last chord (C major) as a whole note.

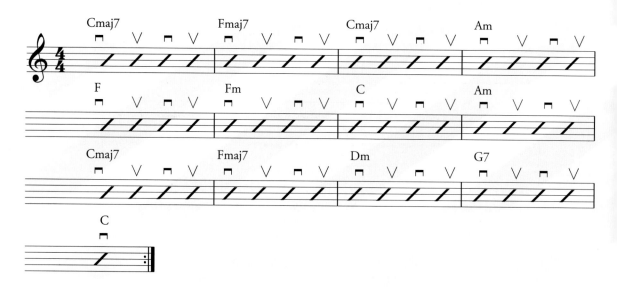

THE **F MINOR** CHORD

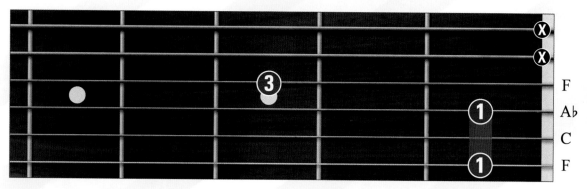

C MAJOR SEVENTH

1st position

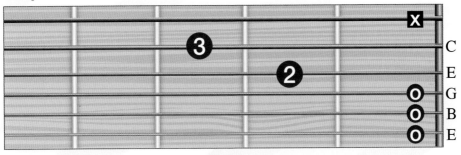

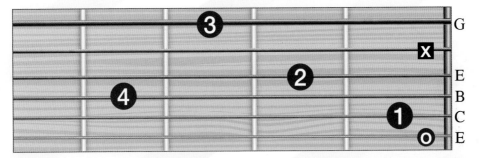

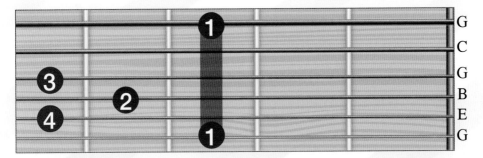

Fret 7

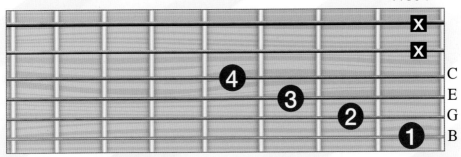

1st position

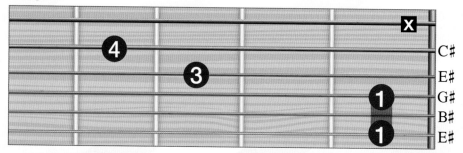

C#
E#
G#
B#
E#

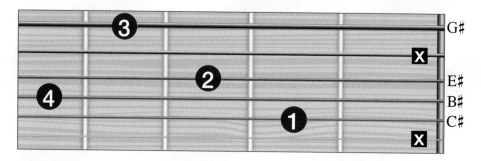

G#
E#
B#
C#

Fret 4

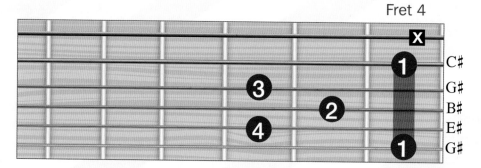

C#
G#
B#
E#
G#

Fret 6

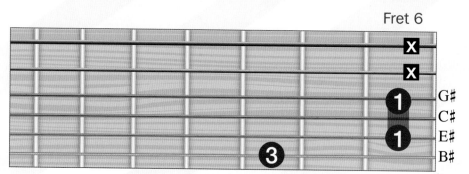

G#
C#
E#
B#

D MAJOR SEVENTH

1st position

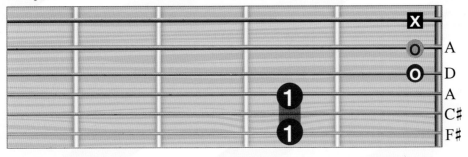

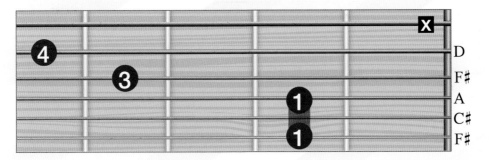

Fret 5

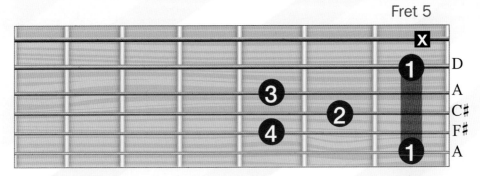

Fret 7

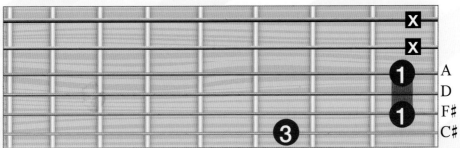

1st position

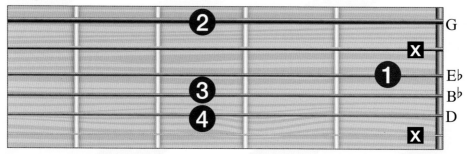

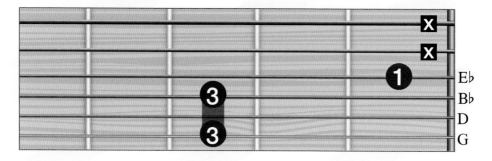

Fret 3

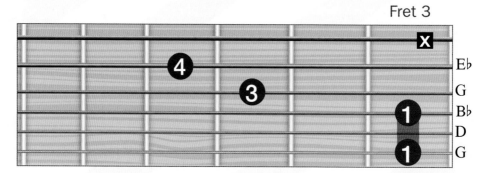

Fret 6

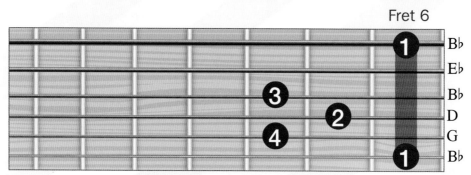

1st position

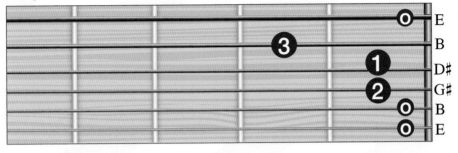

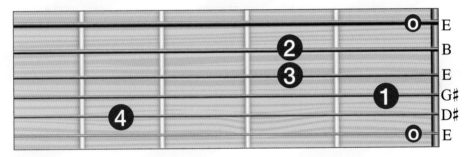

Fret 4

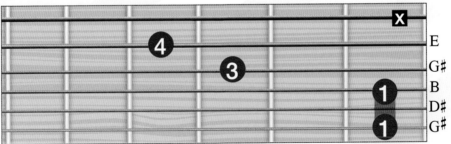

Fret 7

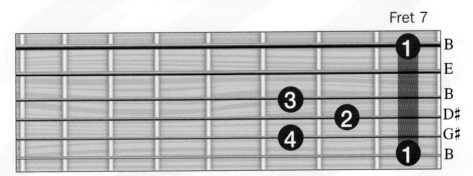

1st position

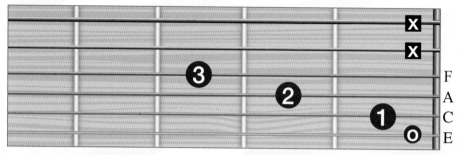

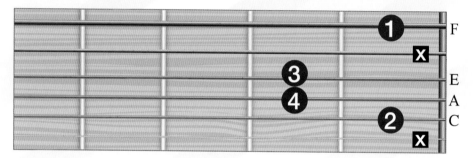

Fret 3

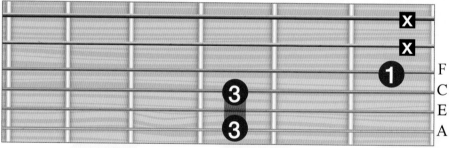

Fret 5

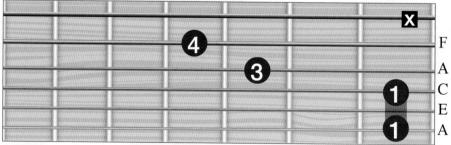

1st position

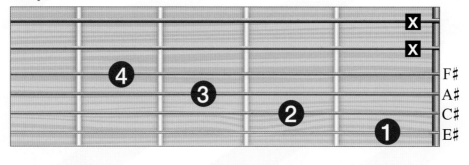

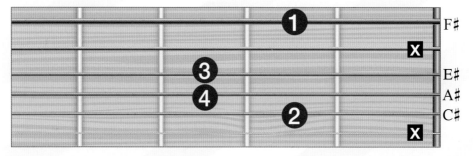

Fret 4

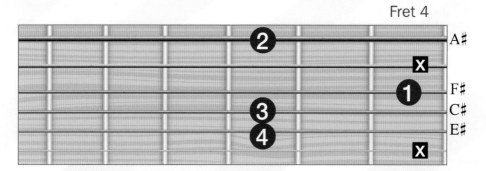

Fret 6

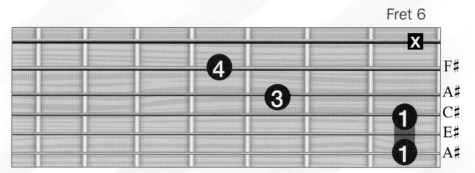

1st position

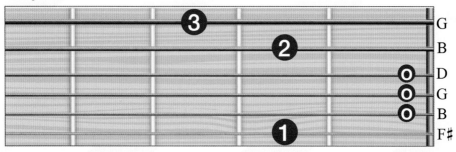

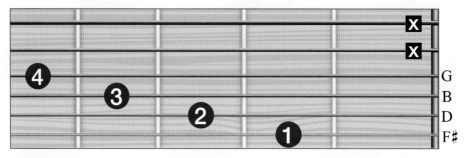

Fret 3

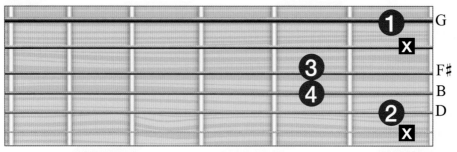

Fret 5

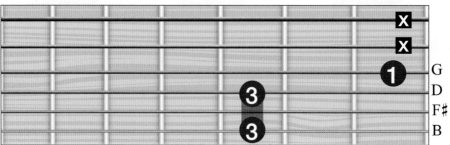

(G♯) A♭ MAJOR SEVENTH

1st position

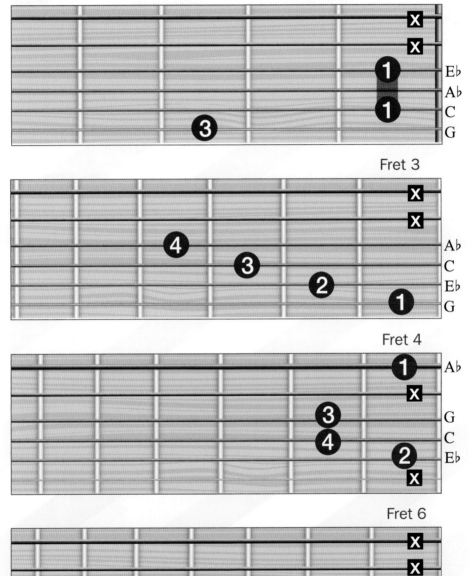

Fret 3

Fret 4

Fret 6

1st position

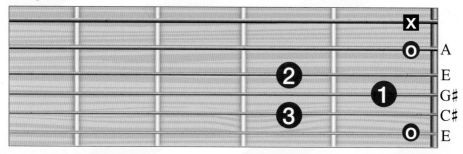

X
A — O
E — 2
G# — 1
C# — 3
E — O

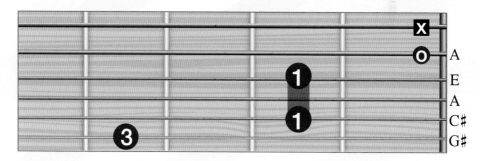

X
A — O
E — 1
A — 1
C# — 1
G# — 3

Fret 4

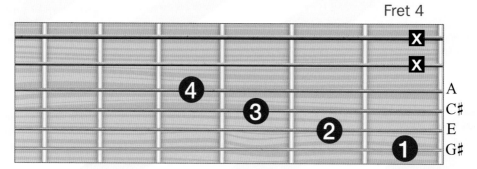

X
X
A — 4
C# — 3
E — 2
G# — 1

Fret 5

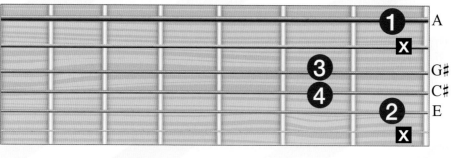

A — 1
X
G# — 3
C# — 4
E — 2
X

(A♯) B♭ MAJOR SEVENTH

1st position

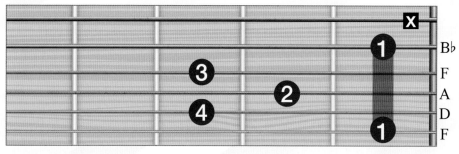

Bb
F
A
D
F

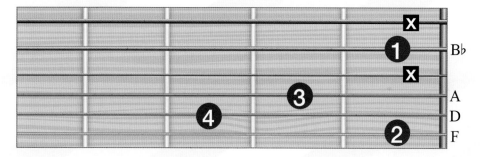

Bb
A
D
F

Fret 5

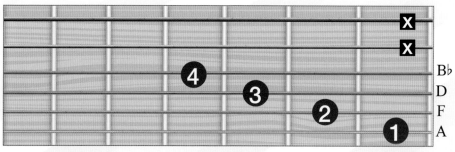

Bb
D
F
A

Fret 6

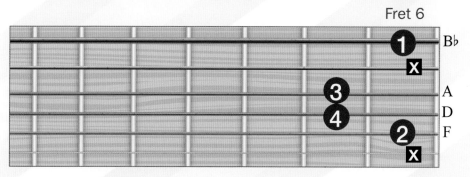

Bb
A
D
F

1st position

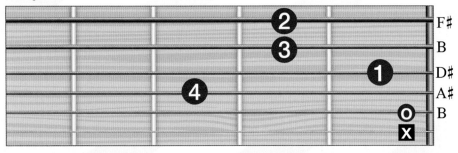

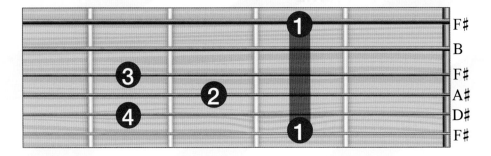

Fret 4

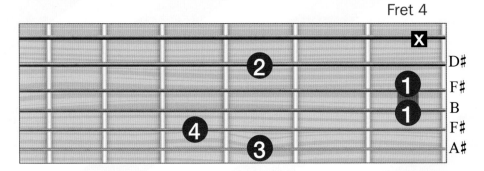

Fret 6

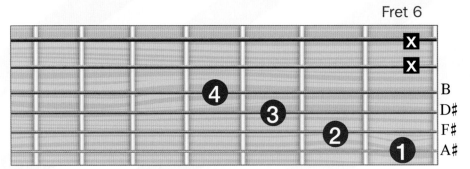

Minor sevenths don't sound as lush as major sevenths, and they don't have the strong mood of minor chords. In fact, they sound a little abstract. Interestingly, minor sevenths are frequently found in Latin, Afro-Cuban, and Brazilian jazz forms. It's a chord that works well against those creative and driving rhythms. That said, you can add them to any musical style to add a bit of edge and mystery.

THE A MINOR SEVENTH CHORD

The Am7 chord can be played in two ways in the first position. The easiest way is to make the Am chord and lift your third finger. The other way is to make an Am chord and add your fourth finger to the third fret of the first string.

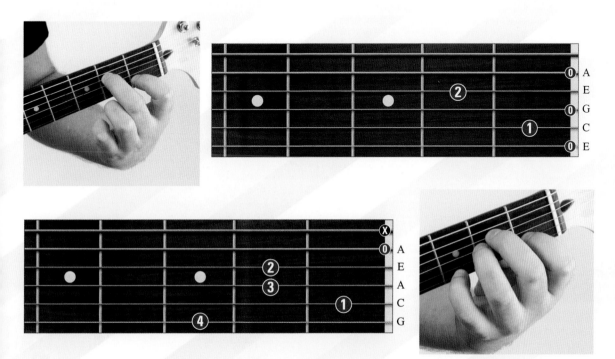

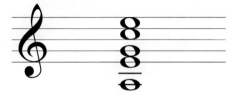

CHORD FINGERING REVIEW

The chord progression on the next page is a bit tricky. It uses some chords you learned a while ago. Make sure you refamiliarize yourself with these finger positions before giving this progression a try!

E MINOR CHORD

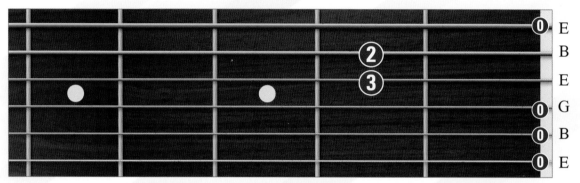

D DOMINANT SEVENTH CHORD

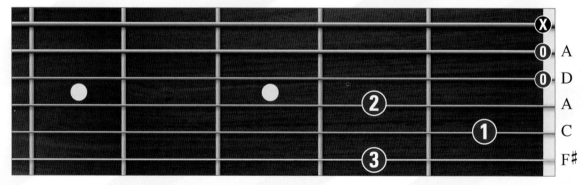

Now let's add Am7 to a progression.

THE D MINOR SEVENTH CHORD

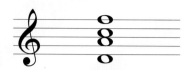

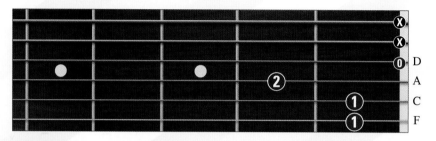

D
A
C
F

THE E MINOR SEVENTH CHORD

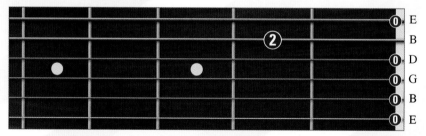

E
B
D
G
B
E

ALL THREE TOGETHER

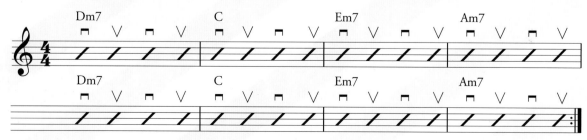

Dm7   C   Em7   Am7

Dm7   C   Em7   Am7

Now let's try something really challenging. This progression features four chord types: major, minor, major seventh, and minor seventh.

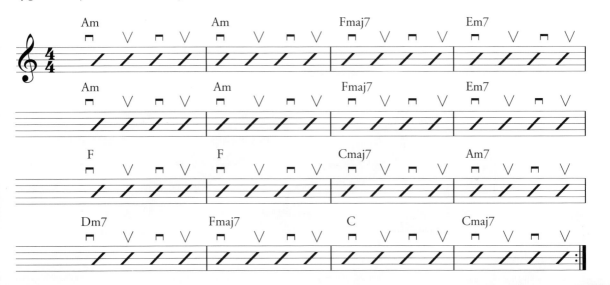

UKULELE

During the nineteenth century, musicians in Hawaii came up with the ukulele, their own version of the small guitars that were coming to the islands with settlers from Spain and Portugal. The baritone ukulele is a great instrument for children who want to learn the guitar. It has soft strings that are easy on a beginner's fingers.

CHORD TOOLBOX REVIEW

Let's revisit the dominant seventh chords. Note how these chords,
when combined with major chords, add a nice twist to the progression.

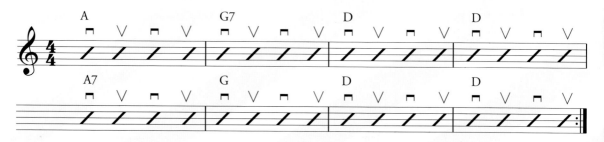

And in this progression, note how the dominant sevenths and minor
chords affect each other.

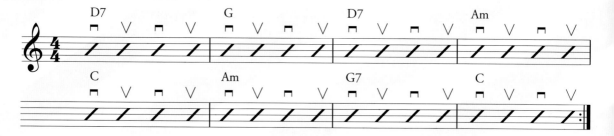

FROM CHORD PROGRESSION TO SONG

Congratulations—your chord repertoire has grown large enough to allow you to play a wide variety of songs. You're ready to put progressions together to make verses and choruses.

Let's learn this chord progression and use it as the verse of a simple song. It's an eight-bar sequence that is repeated once.

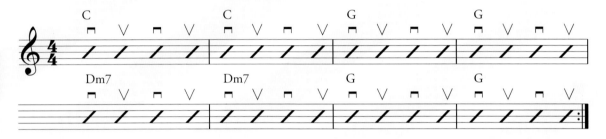

And let's learn this chord progression and use it as the chorus for the song. It's an eight-bar sequence that is played only once. Once you're comfortable with both progressions, turn the page to play them together.

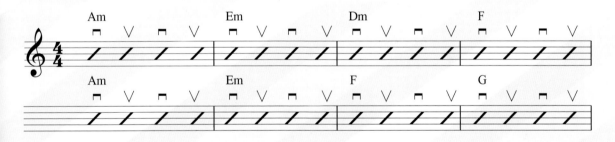

Play the verse and chorus as one song. When you get to the end of the eighth bar, play once more from the beginning. Then go on to the chorus. When you get to the very last bar (the end of the chorus), you'll see D.C. written below it. It's an abbreviation of the Italian words *Da Capo* ("from the head"), and it means to go back and repeat the music once more from the beginning.

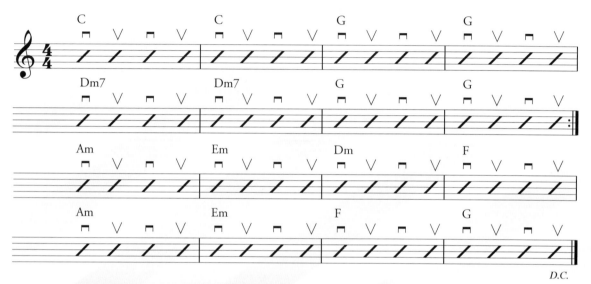

D.C.

THE SG

Gibson introduced the SG in 1961. It's a no-frills guitar great for playing rock 'n' roll. The double-cutaway design allows easy access to the highest frets.

1st position

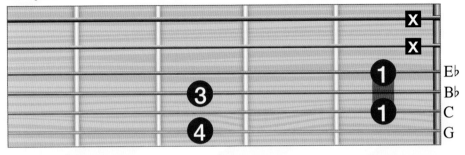

E♭
B♭
C
G

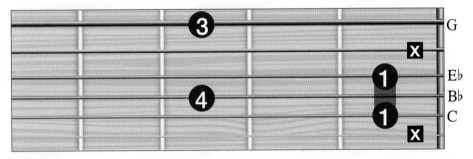

G
E♭
B♭
C

Fret 3

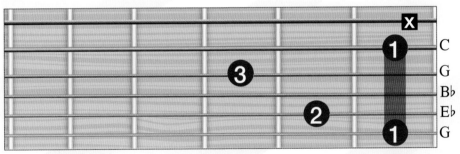

C
G
B♭
E♭
G

Fret 7

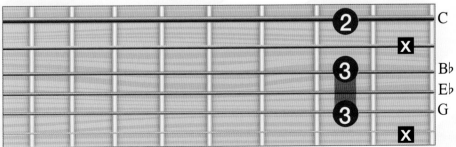

C
B♭
E♭
G

C# (Db) MINOR SEVENTH

1st position

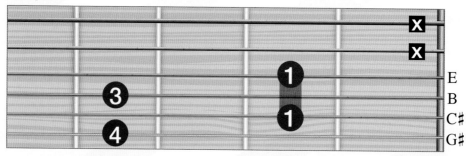

E
B
C#
G#

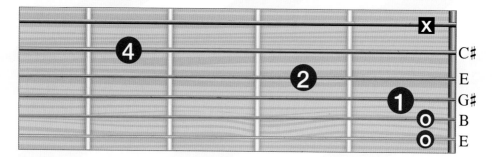

C#
E
G#
B
E

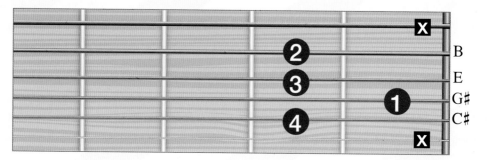

B
E
G#
C#

Fret 4

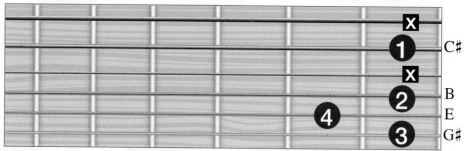

C#
B
E
G#

1st position

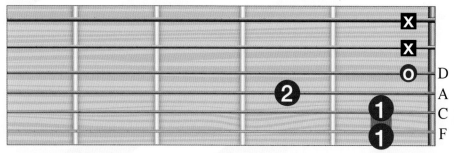

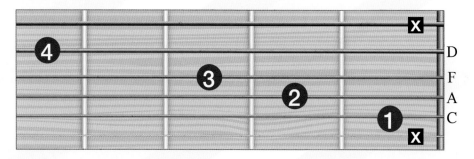

Fret 3

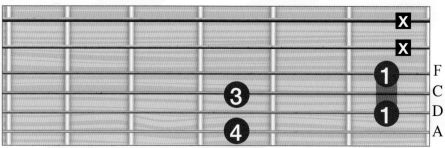

Fret 5

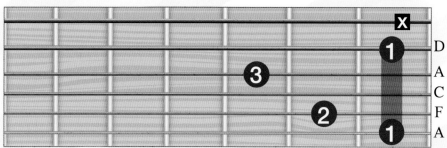

1st position

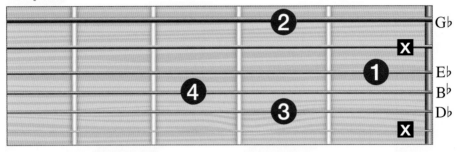

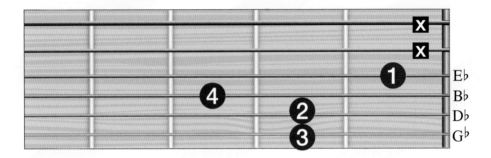

Fret 4

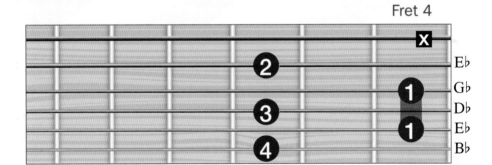

Fret 6

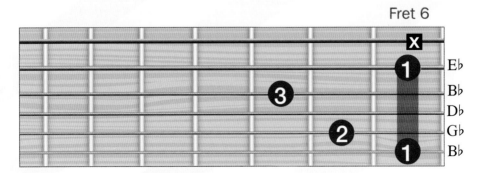

1st position

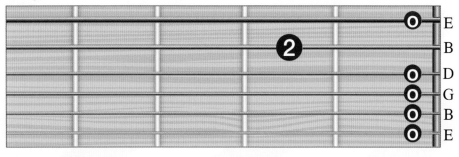

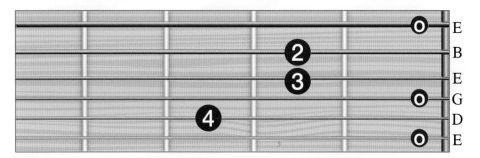

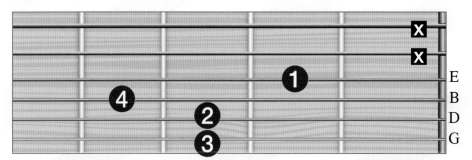

Fret 5

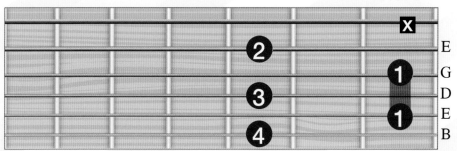

1st position

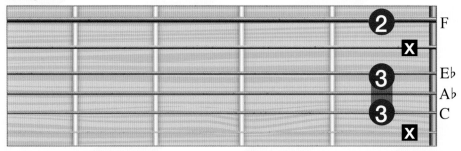

F
X
E♭
A♭
C
X

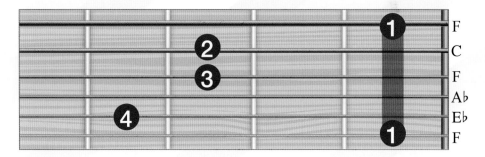

F
C
F
A♭
E♭
F

Fret 4

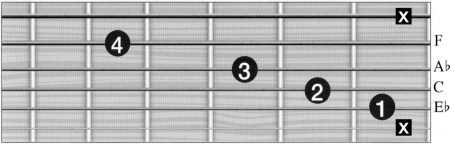

X
F
A♭
C
E♭
X

Fret 6

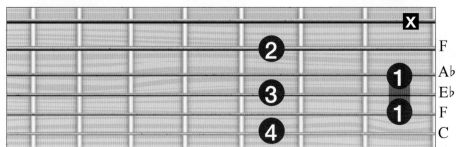

X
F
A♭
E♭
F
C

1st position

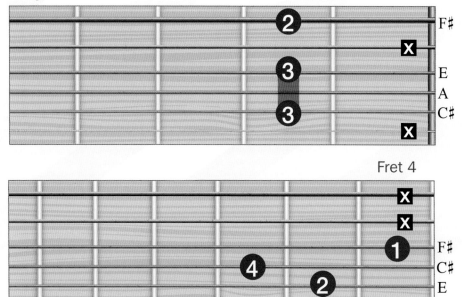

Fret 4

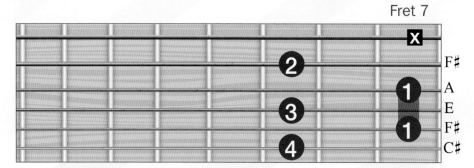

Fret 7

Fret 9

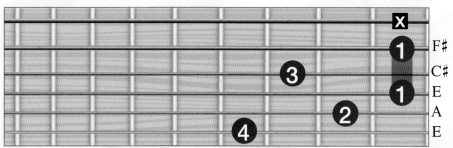

1st position

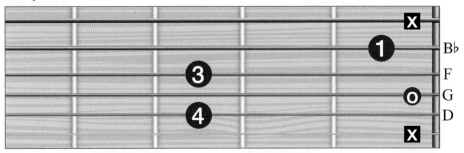

X
1 — B♭
3 — F
O — G
4 — D
X

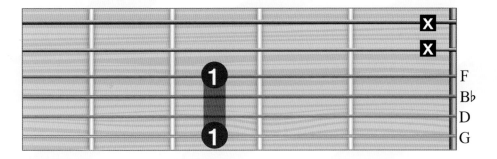

X
X
1 — F
— B♭
— D
1 — G

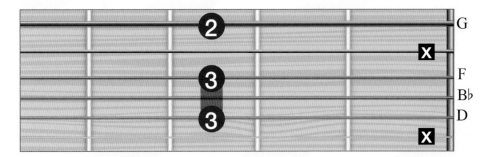

2 — G
X
3 — F
3 — B♭
— D
X

Fret 3

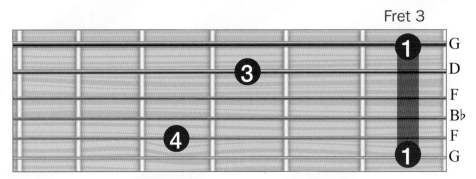

1 — G
3 — D
— F
— B♭
4 — F
1 — G

(G♯) A♭ MINOR SEVENTH

1st position

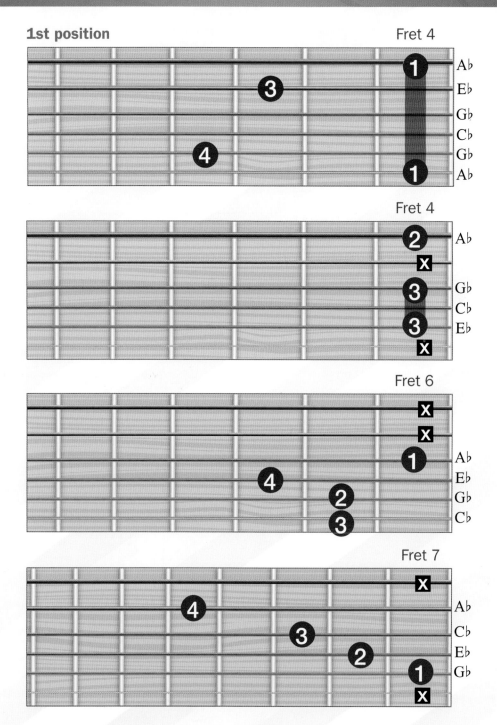

Fret 4

Fret 4

Fret 6

Fret 7

A MINOR SEVENTH

1st position

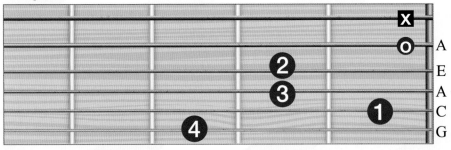

X
o A
2 E
3 A
1 C
4 G

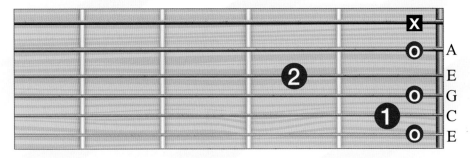

X
o A
2 E
o G
1 C
o E

Fret 5

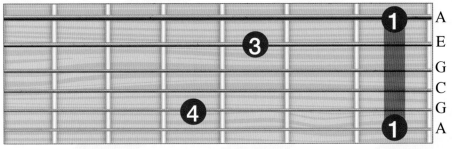

1 A
3 E
G
C
4 G
1 A

Fret 7

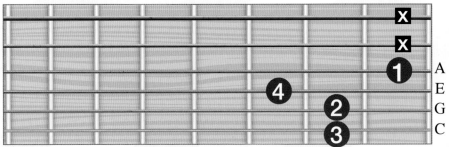

X
X
1 A
4 E
2 G
3 C

1st position

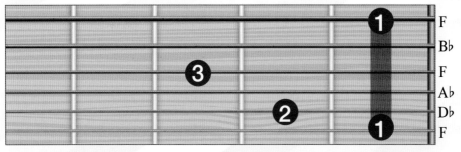

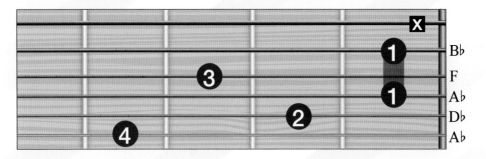

Fret 6

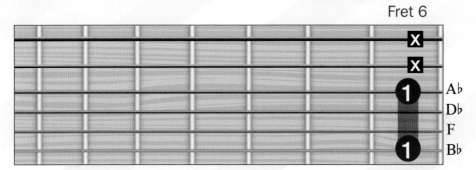

Fret 6

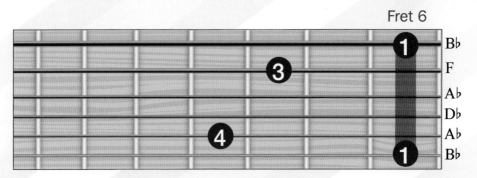

1st position

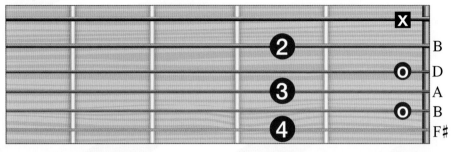

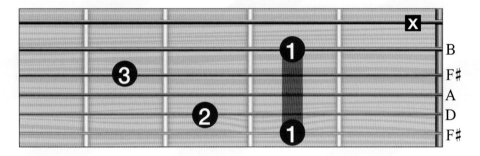

Fret 3

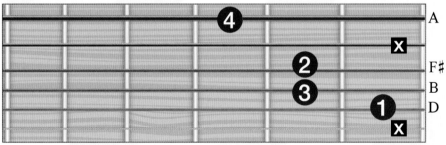

Fret 7

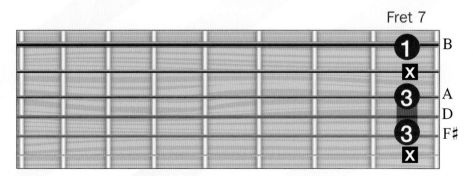

These are chords that know where they're going. They want to resolve into other chords. Think of the related word, "suspense." Most of the time, the suspended fourth will give the listener a feeling of suspense and a sense that the progression needs to move along and change.

THE **A SUSPENDED** FOURTH CHORD

THE **D SUSPENDED** FOURTH CHORD

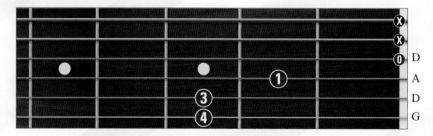

THE E SUSPENDED FOURTH CHORD

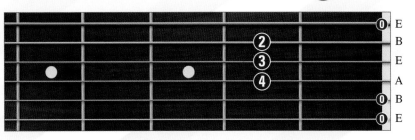

					O	E
				2		B
				3		E
●			●	4		A
					O	B
					O	E

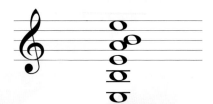

THE C SUSPENDED FOURTH CHORD

					X	
			3			C
			4			F
	●		●		O	G
					1	C
					1	E

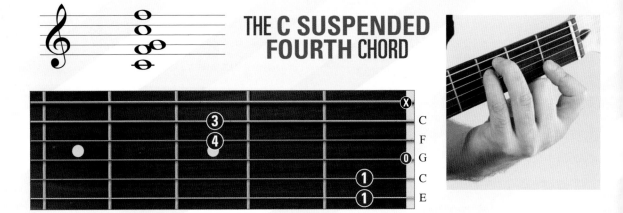

THE F SUSPENDED FOURTH CHORD

					X	
					X	
			3			F
	●		4			Bb
					1	C
					1	F

Note how the sus4 creates a sense of movement in these progressions.

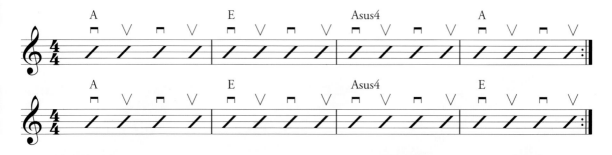

This progression uses four different chord types for an upbeat, active effect.

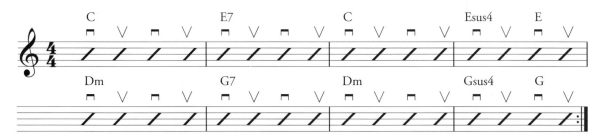

There's a new sus4 in this progression: Gsus4.

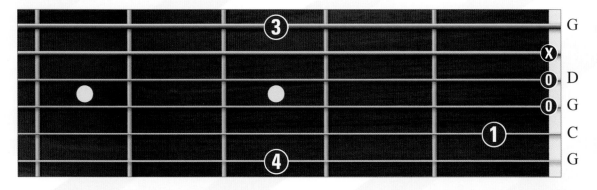

While it's common to hear a suspended fourth resolve into its major equivalent in a chord progression, you'll hear it used in other ways too. Sometimes a sus4 will move to an unexpected chord, and this can give the progression an unsettled feeling.

1st position

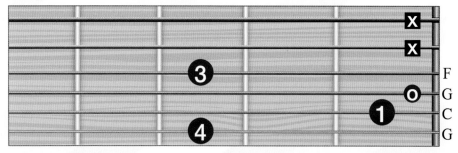

F
G
C
G

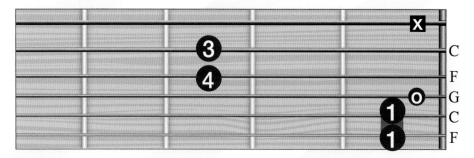

C
F
G
C
F

Fret 3

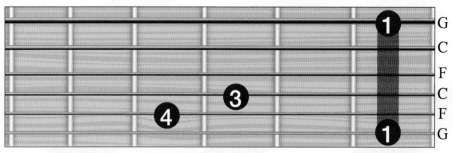

G
C
F
C
F
G

Fret 5

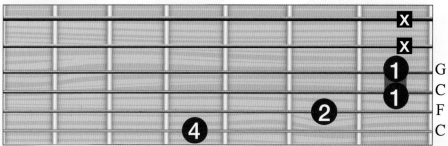

G
C
F
C

1st position

Fret 4

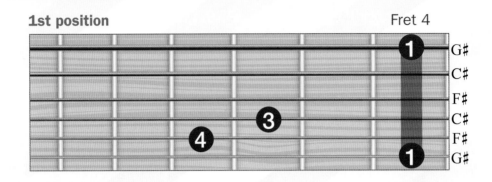

G#
C#
F#
C#
F#
G#

Fret 4

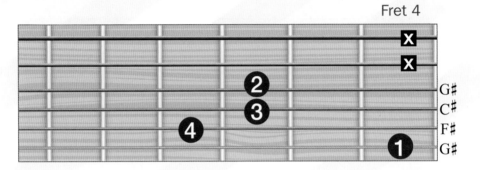

G#
C#
F#
G#

Fret 6

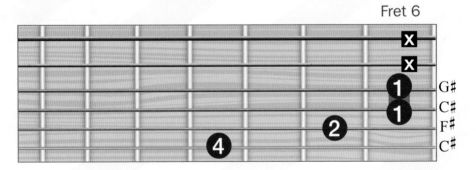

G#
C#
F#
C#

Fret 9

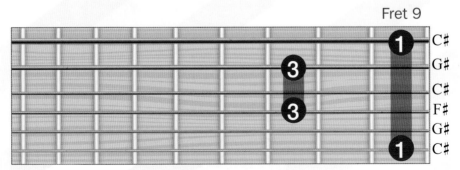

C#
G#
C#
F#
G#
C#

1st position

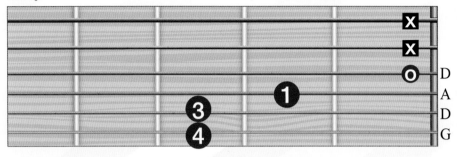

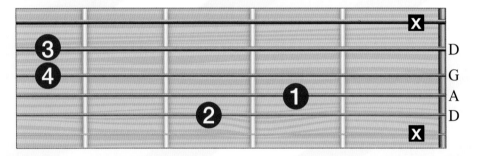

Fret 5

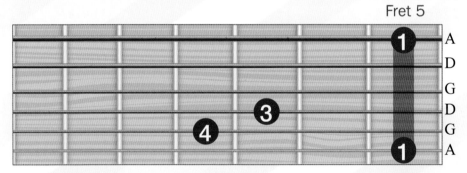

Fret 7

(D♯) E♭ SUSPENDED FOURTH

1st position

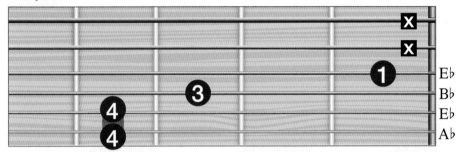

Eb
Bb
Eb
Ab

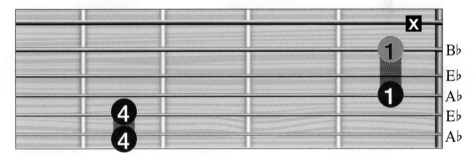

Bb
Eb
Ab
Eb
Ab

Fret 3

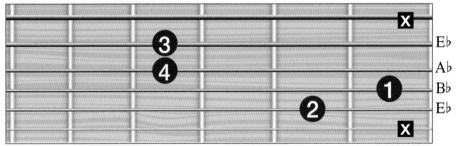

Eb
Ab
Bb
Eb

Fret 6

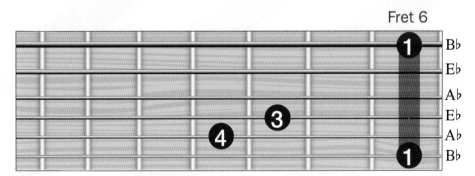

Bb
Eb
Ab
Eb
Ab
Bb

1st position

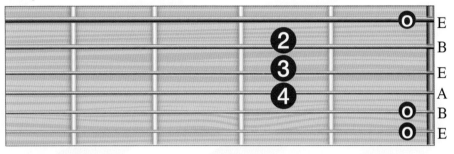

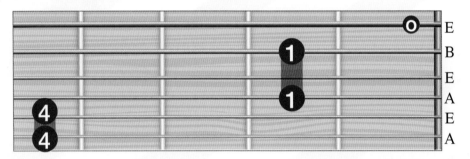

Fret 4

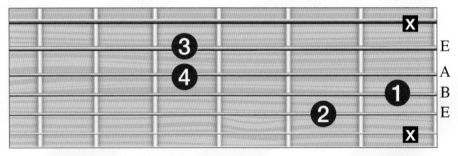

Fret 7

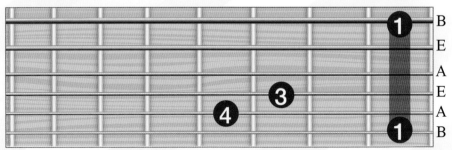

1st position

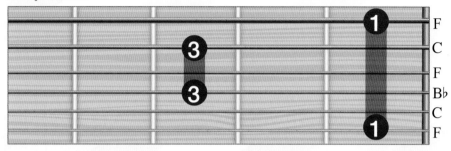

F
C
F
B♭
C
F

Fret 3

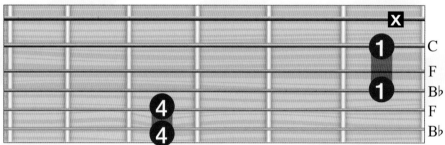

C
F
B♭
F
B♭

Fret 3

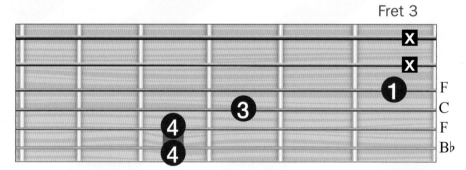

F
C
F
B♭

Fret 8

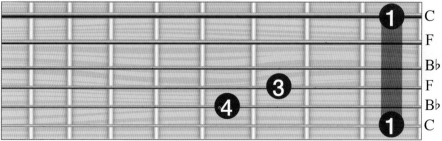

C
F
B♭
F
B♭
C

F♯ (G♭) SUSPENDED FOURTH

1st position

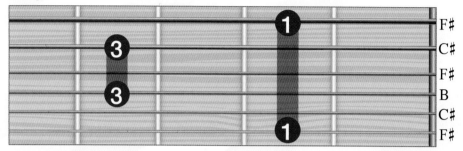

Fret 4

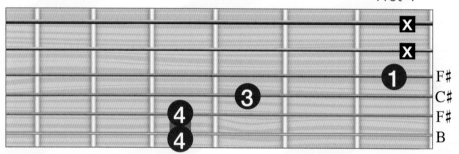

Fret 6

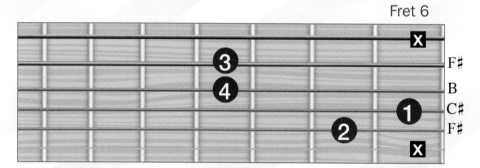

Fret 6

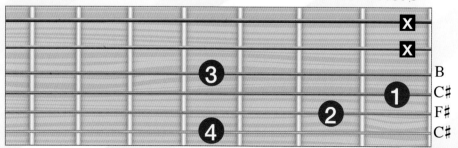

1st position

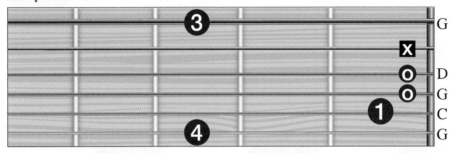

G
x
D
G
C
G

Fret 3

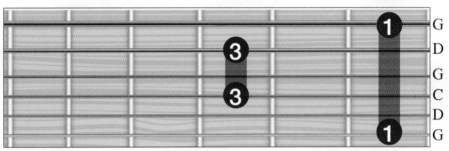

G
D
G
C
D
G

Fret 5

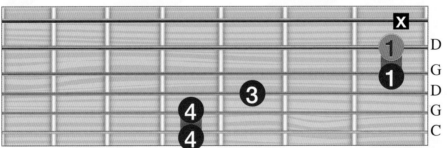

x
D
G
D
G
C

Fret 7

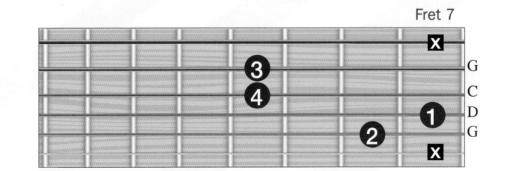

x
G
C
D
G
x

1st position

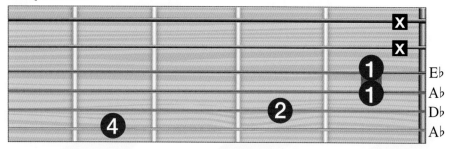

Fret 4

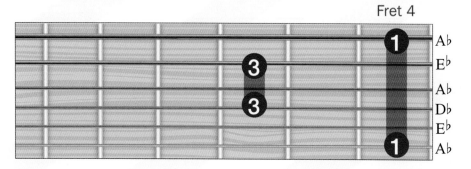

Fret 6

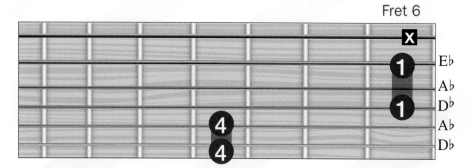

Fret 8

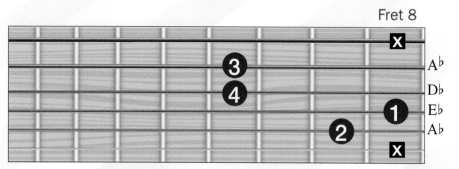

1st position

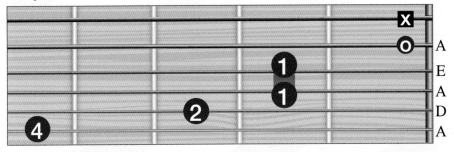

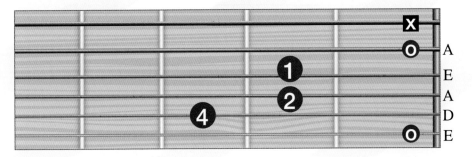

Fret 5

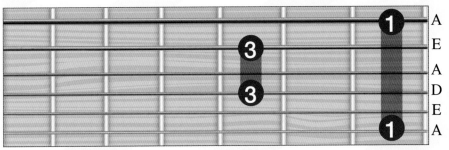

Fret 7

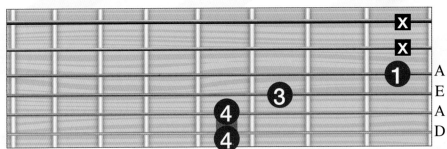

(A♯) B♭ SUSPENDED FOURTH

1st position

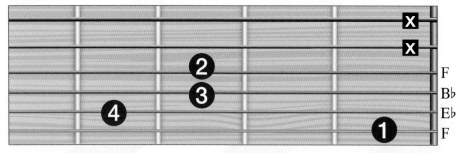

F
B♭
E♭
F

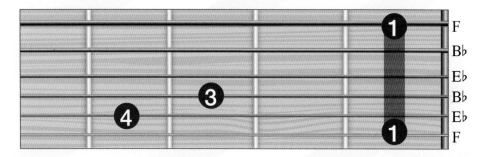

F
B♭
E♭
B♭
E♭
F

Fret 6

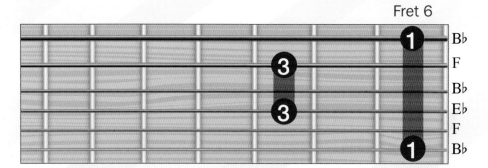

B♭
F
B♭
E♭
F
B♭

Fret 8

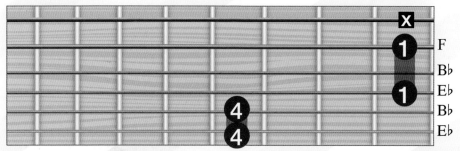

F
B♭
E♭
B♭
E♭

1st position

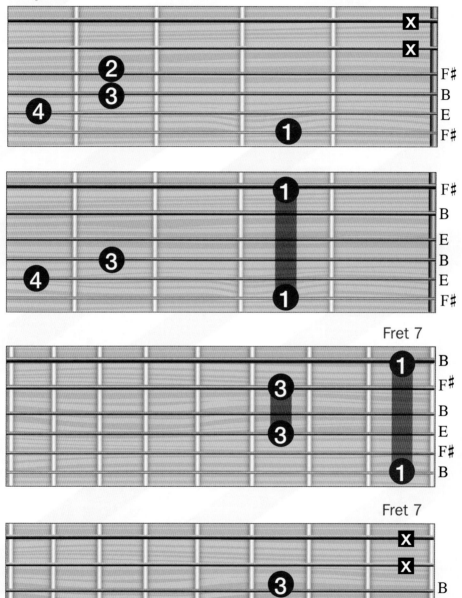

Fret 7

Fret 7

You might say a suspended second is like a thought in passing. As with suspended fourths, these chords imply movement.

THE **A SUSPENDED SECOND** CHORD

THE **D SUSPENDED SECOND** CHORD

THE **C** SUSPENDED SECOND CHORD

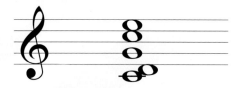

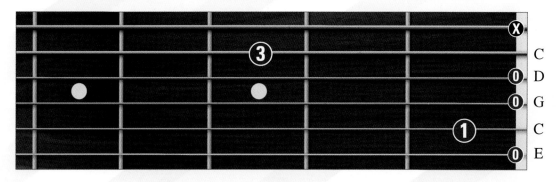

					X	
		③				C
					0	D
●		●			0	G
				①		C
					0	E

THE **F** SUSPENDED SECOND CHORD

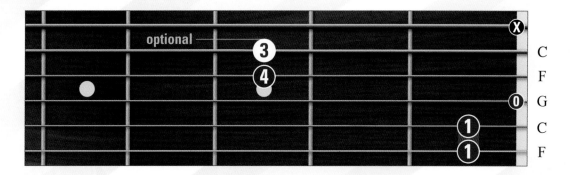

					X	
optional		③				C
		④				F
●		●			0	G
				①		C
				①		F

Here's a short, folksy-sounding progression featuring the Dsus4 and Dsus2. Notice what's going on in the third bar!

Now let's use the sus2 chord as part of a four-bar introduction. We'll add this introduction to the song below.

And now let's add a new wrinkle: a song with an introduction. The song will be repeated but the introduction will be played just once. There is a new repeat symbol in the notation that indicates this.

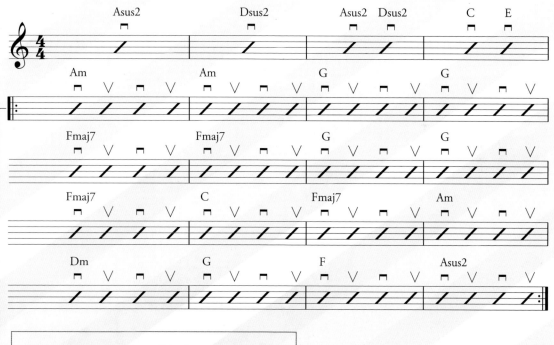

This repeat bar indicates the place you go back to when you reach the ending repeat sign.

Here's another song with an introduction that only gets played once. Some of the changes here are both fast and tricky. Be prepared for a finger workout!

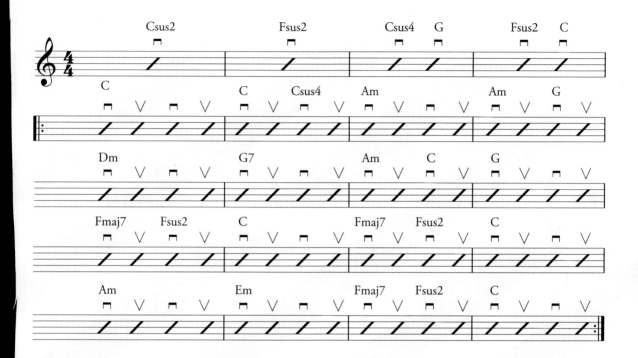

LUTE

Before the development of the modern guitar, musicians played similar-looking string instruments like the vihuela and the gittern. The lute was another early predecessor. It became a popular instrument during the Renaissance, both as a solo instrument and in small ensembles. Lutes had a variable number of strings—some as many as 24.

Our final song switches between two time signatures: the four bars of $\frac{4}{4}$ act as the bridge between the verse and chorus. The rest of the song is in $\frac{3}{4}$. Note how some of the sus4 chords don't resolve, giving some movement and tension to the progression.